PUBLICATIONS OF THE

FOUNDATION FOR FINNISH ASSYRIOLOGICAL RESEARCH

NO. 9

STATE ARCHIVES OF ASSYRIA CUNEIFORM TEXTS

VOLUME IX

State Archives of Assyria Cuneiform Texts (SAACT) is a series of text editions presenting central pieces of Mesopotamian literature both in cuneiform and in transliteration, with complete glossaries, name indexes and sign lists generated electronically from the transliterations. The goal of the series is to eventually make the entire library of Assurbanipal available in this format.

Published with the support of the
Foundation for
Finnish Assyriological Research

Set in Times
Typography and layout by Teemu Lipasti
Typesetting by Takayoshi Oshima and Simo Parpola
The Assyrian Royal Seal emblem drawn by Dominique Collon from original
Seventh Century B.C. impressions (BM 84672 and 84677) in the British Museum
Cover: Neo-Assyrian cylinder seal (BM 89810), courtesy Trustees of the British Museum

Printed in the USA and distributed by Eisenbrauns,
Winona Lake, Indiana 46590, USA
www.eisenbrauns.com

ISBN-10 952-10-1343-5 (Volume 9)
ISBN-13 978-952-10-1343-0 (Volume 9)
ISSN 1455-2345 (SAACT)
ISSN 1798-7431 (PFFAR)

STATE ARCHIVES OF ASSYRIA
CUNEIFORM TEXTS
VOLUME IX

THE BABYLONIAN THEODICY

INTRODUCTION, CUNEIFORM TEXT AND TRANSLITERATION
WITH A TRANSLATION, GLOSSARY AND COMMENTARY

By
Takayoshi Oshima

THE NEO-ASSYRIAN TEXT CORPUS PROJECT
2013

In memory of W. G. Lambert (†2011)

ACKNOWLEDGEMENTS

The publication of the *Babylonian Theodicy* and other so-called Babylonian Wisdom Literature has been my ongoing DFG project based at the Friedrich-Schiller Universität Jena since 2010. I would like to thank the Deutsche Forschungsgemeinschaft for financially supporting my project and Prof. Manfred Krebernik, the director of the Altorientalisches Institut of the Friedrich-Schiller-Universität Jena, for his help in numerous matters.

In terms of its grammar and content, the *Babylonian Theodicy* is one of the most difficult Babylonian poems extant. Thus, for the convenience of the reader, it has been decided to provide a brief discussion of the poem and short philological notes in addition to the customary contents of the SAACT series, namely transliteration, translation, glossary, index, and sign list. I have prepared the composite text on the basis of published and unpublished manuscripts which I had already collated or copied from the original tablets with the generous permission of the Trustees of the British Museum and of Dr Joachim Marzahn, curator of the Vorderasiatisches Museum. To all of them, I extend my thanks. The new materials and collations of the published manuscripts will appear at a later date in my comprehensive study of the *Babylonian Theodicy* and other so-called Babylonian wisdom literature.

I would like to thank Prof. Simo Parpola for providing me with all the assistance needed to have this book completed and published. I am also grateful to Prof. Michael P. Streck, Prof. Jan Dietrich, and Dr Uri Gabbay for their critical reading of the manuscript and for their remarks and corrections. I am also in debt to Dr Irving L. Finkel for his assistance. This book also owes much to Dr Thomas Riplinger who not only edited my text but also gave me many constructive and insightful comments. He too is thanked.

All errors of omission or commission remaining in the book are mine alone.

Jena, May 2012 T. Oshima

TABLE OF CONTENTS

Table of Contents

INTRODUCTION[*]

The ancient text known among modern scholars as the *Babylonian Theodicy*[1] is a poem in the form of a dialogue between two learned men. The first figure is customarily called the 'sufferer' because he describes himself as being a victim of social injustice.[2] Modern scholars normally designate the second speaker, who apparently tries to comfort him and advocates worship of the gods, as a 'friend', because, in the dialogue, he is often addressed as *ibrī*, 'my friend,' and *rūʾa*, 'my colleague.' Probably, however, this second speaker represents someone who is older and more learned than the sufferer.

Zimmern and Strong[3] independently of each other published the first hand copies of three exemplars of the Babylonian Theodicy (BM 34773 = Sp II 265a; K 3452 (+) 8463 (+) 8491;[4] 9290+ 9297) with transliteration in 1895. Craig, whose copies of some manuscripts also appeared in the same year, believed that it was a hymn.[5] In 1924, E. Ebeling noted that ethics and social justice are the main themes of the poem.[6] However, he failed to notice the existence of a second speaker and thus concluded that the poem was a lamentation. Dhorme recognized, for the first time, the text's dialogue form.[7] The modern title, the *Babylonian Theodicy*, goes back to B. Landsberger's critical edition of this ancient work in his article, "Die babylonische Theodizee (akrostichisches Zwiegespräch; sog. 'Kohelet')", *ZA* 43 (1936), pp. 32–76,[8] which laid the grounds for the modern understanding of this text. In 1960, in his monumental work, *Babylonian Wisdom Literature*,[9] W. G. Lambert published a new critical text edition together with new copies of all the manuscripts known to him. Since then, Lambert's edition has

---

[*] When I refer to the texts outside of the *Babylonian Theodicy*, I have for the most part based my transliterations and translations on the text-editions established by other scholars. Yet, the readers are advised to bear in mind that I have occasionally altered their readings and renderings when alternations are called for.

[1] The complete incipit, i.e., the ancient title of this poem, has yet to be discovered. Following LAMBERT 1960, p. 70, I restore the first word of the poem based on the first word of the *Theodicy Commentary*. The fact that *a-šiš* is also attested in the colophon of the *Theodicy Commentary* confirms that it was the incipit of the poem. The colophon of the *Theodicy Commentary* reads: [*ṣa*]-⸢*a*⸣-*tú u šu-ut* KA *maš-a-a-al-tú* ^{lú}*um-man-nu šá a-š*[*iš* … *ga-na* [*lu*]-*uq-bi-ka*] *im-gì-di* $^{\text{m d}}$+AG-MU-MU A *šá* $^{\text{m d}}$+A[G- …, 'lexical commentary and oral explanations of questions put to a scholar regarding 'Wise o[ne, ..., come, let me tell you ...]' one-column tablet, (property) of Nabû-šuma-iddina, the son of Na[bû- …].'

[2] MATTINGLY 1990, p. 325 calls him "skeptic."

[3] ZIMMERN 1895 and STRONG 1895. In the same year (1895), copies of the same tables also appeared in CRAIG, *ABRT* I, pp. 43–53.

[4] Neither of them noticed that K 3452 (+) 8463 (+) 8491 belonged to one exemplar.

[5] *ABRT* I, p. VII.

[6] EBELING 1924, p. 1. He also used KAR 160 (=VAT 10567).

[7] DHORME 1923.

[8] = LANDSBERGER 1936.

[9] = LAMBERT 1960. The transliteration and translation = pp. 63–89; commentaries = pp. 302–310; hand-copies = pls. 19–26.

served, as the base of modern studies of this *Babylonian Theodicy*. The most recent full text edition, accompanied by an Italian translation, is that of PONCHIA 1996.[10] Diverse scholars have offered various translations of this difficult ancient poem. The most notable examples are: BIGGS 1969, pp. 601–604; LABAT 1970, pp. 320–327; VON SODEN 1990, pp. 143–157; and FOSTER 2005, pp. 914–922.[11] Although these translations are also intended for non-Assyriologists, they contain — particularly von Soden's work — many useful notes that have contributed to the understanding of this difficult poem. Because of its motif resembling the *Book of Job* of the Bible, the *Babylonian Theodicy* has also been discussed by different scholars in the field of the biblical studies, theology, and the studies of religions of Ancient Near East.[12]

Nine manuscripts are currently known to me.[13] All of these manuscripts are from the first millennium, either in Neo-Assyrian or Neo-/Late-Babylonian scripts.[14] The date of the original composition, however, could well be considerably earlier and thus, tentatively, I offer a late second millennium BCE dating.[15] Based on the extant manuscripts of the poem itself, together with the manuscript of an ancient commentary on the *Babylonian Theodicy* from the Late-Babylonian period, which was found at Borsippa or Sippar (referred to below as the *Theodicy Commentary*), BM 66882 + 76506 + 76009 + 76832 + 83044 + 83045 + 83046,[16] it is now possible to recover fully or in part some 272 lines out of a presumed to-

---

[10] PONCHIA 1996, translation = pp. 73–82; transliteration = pp. 101–108; and notes = pp. 131–142.

[11] BOTTÉRO 1977, pp. 28–38 also offers his French translation of the *Babylonian Theodicy* in his study on the question of adversity and the "juste suouffrant."

[12] Because of its popularity, it is simply impossible to cite here each single reference to the *Babylonian Theodicy* in the comparative studies with the *Book of Job*. For recent discussions of the *Babylonian Theodicy* in comparison with the *Book of Job* with an up-to-date bibliography, see, VAN DER TOORN 2003, pp. 64–76; UEHLINGER 2007, pp. 146–159. Uehlinger also offers his German translation of the portions of the *Babylonian Theodicy* relevant to his discussion. Leaving aside the biblical book's opening narrative and the problem of its different endings, there are obvious parallels between the debate between the Babylonian 'sufferer' and 'friend' and the biblical debate between Job and his 'comforters'. Both protagonists, the sufferer of the *Babylonian Theodicy* and Job, bewail the ways in which the divine beings have responded to their piety and question divine justice. The friend in the *Babylonian Theodicy* and the four counsellors in the *Book of Job* both offer advice based on belief in divine justice and retribution. Creation stories are also used to explain (or at least intend to explain) the *conditio humana* in both poems. Yet, there are also striking differences between them. Probably the most evident difference is the reasons why the discourses are engaged in — while Job bewails his undeserved adversities and God's silence to his allegation of mishandling him, the protagonist of the *Babylonian Theodicy* complains that the will of the gods is opaque and his piety has not been rewarded with prosperity. Like Job, the protagonist of the *Babylonian Theodicy* does not doubt his own righteousness, but, unlike Job, he expresses blasphemous thoughts which must have been considered as sins according to traditional Babylonian belief. See below. Unlike Job, he does not wish to prove his innocence in front of the divine-beings. In any case, this is not the place to discuss in detail the relationship of the *Babylonian Theodicy* to the biblical *Book of Job*. I hope to treat in detail the similarities and differences between the two works in a future publication.

[13] For the manuscripts of the *Babylonian Theodicy*, see p. lii.

[14] LAMBERT 1960, p. 63 dates BM 34633 (MS m of Lambert, MS A in the present volume) to the Seleucid or even Parthian period.

[15] For the question of the authorship and the date of composition, see below.

[16] The joins were made by I. Finkel. OELSNER 1986, p. 227 has suggested a Hellenistic date, probably from Borsippa.

tal 297 lines in all. Yet, because of the significant number of lacunae in the mid sections (lines 89–125; 148–158; 166–181; 191–205; 210–234), many uncertainties remain unresolved.

Remarks on the Literary Style

The *Babylonian Theodicy* consists of 27 strophes of 11 lines each. Remarkably, all the sentences in a single strophe begin with the same sign. When these 27 signs in all are read from the beginning to the end, they form an acrostic.[17] Nevertheless, in constructing this acrostic, the author did not make full use of the polyphonic potential of the cuneiform signs at the beginning of each line. Another interesting observation is that the author also did not use these first signs for logograms (Sumerograms).

In each stanza, one almost always finds an odd line that does not follow the pattern typical for that stanza (e.g., its rhyme).[18] Although the author also employed other devices in order to add dynamism to the otherwise symmetrical and monotonous stanzas, these odd lines act as a kind of 'spice' which gives vitality to the poem. The location of the odd line within a strophe is "unpredictable both structurally and graphically."[19] Judging from the contexts, it seems that it was most often employed "for an emphatic statement."[20]

Most of the lines in this work consist of four units.[21] This is very evident in four manuscripts from Babylon — BM 34773 (MS B), BM 35405 (MS C), BM 47745 (MS E), and BM 68589 (MS F). The scribes of these manuscripts not only drew a horizontal dividing line after each eleven lines but also divided each column into four sections with vertical dividing lines and carefully arranged the words in these 'boxes' in order to set out these units.

In addition to the acrostic, the author repeatedly — often meticulously — used rhymes, probably in order to create certain rhythms.[22] These rhymes are normally located in the initial words of the sentences. For example Strophe XXVI (lines 276–286):

276 *šarri qadmi* ^{d}*narru banû apât*[*um*]
277 *šarḫu* ^{d}*zulummaru kariṣ ṭiṭṭašina*
278 *šarratum pātiqtašina šuʾētu* ^{d}*mami*
279 *šarkū ana amēluttu etguru dabāba*
280 *sarrātu u lā kinātu išrukūšu santakku*

[17] For the acrostic, see below.

[18] See below.

[19] DENNING-BOLLE 1992, p. 139. BUCCELLATI 1972, p. 167 argues that preference is shown for either the third or last line.

[20] LAMBERT 1960, p. 66.

[21] Already noted by ZIMMERN 1895, p. 2.

[22] For a study of the metre in the *Babylonian Theodicy*, see, IZRE'EL 1996. For general discussions on poetic metre in Mesopotamia, see e.g., VON SODEN, 1981; *idem* 1984; and GRONEBERG 1996; REINER 1985, *passim*.

281 *šarḫiš ša šarî idabbubū dumqīšu*
282 *šarmi mešrû illakū idāšu*
283 *šarrāqiš ulammanū dunnamâ amēlū*
284 *šarkūš nullâtum ikappudūšu nērti*
285 *sarriš kala lumnū šūḫuzūšu aššu lā išû irītu*
286 *šarbābiš ušḫarammûšu uballûšu kīma lāmi*

The first signs of the first three couplets contain the sequence of *š/sarr–šarḫ/k/q* until line 282. Also in line 282, the author follows this pattern, beginning it with *šar-mi* (i.e., *šarru* + *mi*), but, in line 283, he breaks the sequence by *šarraqiš*. This is followed, however, by another couplet (lines 284–285) with the same rhyme but in a reverse order, *šark–sarr*. The last sentence, line 286, is the odd line of this strophe which does not follow the rhymes.

Another example is the first words of Strophe II, where the author repeats the *nad/ṭ–nar* sequence for three couplets. He then breaks this pattern by repeating the syllable <*naṭ*> instead of the expected syllable <*nar*> in line 19 and reverses the order (i.e., *naṭ–nar*) in the following couplet. He also concludes this stanza with an odd line, beginning with the syllable <*naq*>.

More careful observation of Strophe XXVI, which will be discussed above, reveals that the last quatrain (lines 283–286), which speaks of the horrible destiny of the poor/fool, is marked off as a single unit by a metre arranged more closely than the *š/sarr–šarḫ/k/q* alliteration discussed above — here the first words rhyme not only at the beginning but also at the end, i.e. the ending <*š*>; there are also consonances involving the sounds combinations <*l*>...<*m*>; and rhymes between *ikappudūšu nērti* and *išû irītu* of lines 284–285:

283 *šarrāqiš ulammanū dunnamâ amēlū*
284 *šarkūš nullâtum ikappudūšu nērti*
285 *sarriš kala lumnū šūḫuūšu aššu lā išû irītu*
286 *šarbābiš ušḫarammûšu uballûšu kīma lāmi*

Given the fact that this quatrain includes the odd line (line 286), it is evident that this section was intended to express the main message of Strophe XXVI. Thus, everywhere in this poem, the author demonstrates remarkable literary skill; so we must ask: who was the author of this poem?

The Author and the Date of Composition

As stated above, all the 11 lines of each stanza begin with the same sign.[23] When we read these signs acrostically, they reveal the name of the author:

a-na-ku sa-ag-gi-il-ki-[i-na-a]m-ub-bi-ib ma-áš-ma-šu ka-ri-bu ša i-li ú šar-ri

[23] ZIMMERN 1895, pp. 15–16 had already surmised that it was an acrostic poem. For a survey of acrostics in cuneiform texts and in the texts from the Bible, see, e.g., SOLL 1988.

'I am Saggil-kīnam-ubbib, an incantation-priest, the one who praises deity and the king.'

This name Saggil-kīnam-ubbib literally means 'O (E)saggil, clear the righteous (of accusation/sins).'[24] Saggil is a short form of Esagil (*é-sag-íla/gíl*), the temple of Marduk in Babylon.[25]

The personal name (E)saggil-kīnam-ubbib is not widely attested in the cuneiform texts known to us. It is difficult to determine its significance, but this name does appear on a Neo-/Late-Babylonian school exercise tablet from Sippar, BM 65649+76479, rev col. iii 4'–7':[26]

4' [^{m}*é-sag-íl*]-*ki-i-ni-ub-bi-ib*
5' ^{m}*é-sag-íl*-DU-*ub-bi-ib*
6' ^{m}*é-sag-íl-ki-i-ni-ub-bi-ib*
7' ^{m}*é-sag-íl*-DU-*ub-bi-ib*

Apparently the purpose of this exercise was to practice different orthographies for the same name.[27]

Similar names are known in a tablet found in Late-Babylonian Uruk.[28] This tablet is a list of ancient kings and their counsellors, who are designated abgal in Sumerian and *ummânu* in Akkadian. The reference to Esarhaddon and his scholar Ahiqar in lines 19–20 suggests a seventh century BCE date as a *terminus post quem* for the compilation of the Uruk list.

Lines 17–18 of the Uruk list read as follows:[29]

17 [During the time of] the king Adad-apla-iddina was the king: Esagil-kīnī-ubba was the scholar.
18 [During the time of] the king Nebuchadnezzar (I) was the king: Esagil-kīnī-ubbalu[30] was the scholar.

Modern scholars normally take these names listed in the Uruk list to be our Saggil-kīnam-ubbib.[31] According to the ancient catalogue of texts and authors from

[24] STAMM 1939, pp. 172–173; VON SODEN 1990, p. 143. *CAD* E, on the other hand, by taking *ub-bib* to be the preterit form of *ebēbu* D-stem, translates "Esagila-Has-Made-the-Just-Clear", *CAD* E, p. 7, *ebēbu*, 2, c), 5'.

[25] GEORGE 1993, pp. 139–140, no. 967. Given this element, LAMBERT 1960, p. 64 has suggested that (E)saggil-kīna-ubbib was a citizen of Babylon. Yet, as I will discuss below, the famous scholar Esagil-kīn-apli was evidently a citizen of Borsippa despite the inclusion of the name of Marduk's temple within his name. See below. Moreover, almost all the persons bearing names with Saggil- who are known from the Neo-Assyrian period (Saggil-aplu-uṣur, Saggil-biʾdi, Saggilia, Saggil-rāmat (hypo. of Ina-(E)saggil-rāmat), Saggil-šarru-uṣur) were residents of Kalhu. *PNA* III/1, p. 1060. In other words, we cannot rely on the element Saggil to determine a person's origin.

[26] GESCHE 2001, p. 493.

[27] Note also Saggil-kīnu-ubbib, a temple-administrator from Dēr, *PNA* III/1, p. 1060.

[28] W 20030, 7 = VAN DIJK 1962, pp. 44–52, Tf 20, a–c and Tf 27. Van Dijk's copy was later published again as VAN DIJK and MAYER 1980, no. 89.

[29] VAN DIJK 1962, p. 45.

[30] It seems that van Dijk takes these Esagil-kīnī-ubba and Esagil-kīnī-ubbalu to be one person and thus transliterates the sign *LU* in superscript; apparently he understands it to be a determinative, *ibid.* Although LU instead of LÚ is possible, judging from the fact that neither agbal nor *ummânu* in the other lines are written with the determinative LÚ (or LU), this interpretation seems less likely. On the other hand, P.-A. Beaulieu is hesitant about their identities and reads *é-sag-gil-ki-i-ni-ub-ba* and *é-sag-gil-ki-i-ni-ub-ba*-LU respectively, BEAULIEU 2007, pp. 13–14.

the library of Assurbanipal, the authorship of many texts is credited to either a *mašmaššu*, 'incantation-priest,' or a *kalû*, 'lamentation-priest,' but these priests are also designated as *ummânu*, i.e. 'scholar, counsellor.'[32] In other words, certain *mašmaššu*-priests were involved not only in performing rituals but also in scholarly activities like teaching. Therefore, it is very likely that the author of the *Babylonian Theodicy* also acted as an *ummânu* although he identifies himself as *mašmaššu* in the acrostic.[33] That speaks in favour of the identification of Esagil-kīnī-ubba and Esagil-kīnī-ubbalu with our Saggil-kīnam-ubbib. Because these entries are placed immediately after Esagil-kīn-apli[34] and because, more importantly, two kings from the Second Dynasty of Isin, Nebuchadnezzar I (1126–1105) and Adad-apla-iddina (1069–1048), are referred to as their contemporaries, one can well surmise that (E)saggil-kīnam-ubbib was an important scholar in the eleventh century BCE.[35]

There is another list that might contribute to identifying the author of the *Babylonian Theodicy* and his lifetime. W. G. Lambert has suggested that the last word of the first line of the *Babylonian Theodicy* is attested on a fragment of the ancient catalogue of ancient compositions from Assurbanipal's library, K 10802 rev 1–2:[36]

1 [... *lu*]-*uq-bi-ka*
2 [*an-nu-ú šá pi-i* ^{m}*saggil-kīnam-ubbib ina tar-ṣi* $^{m\,d}$*adad-apl*]*a-iddina* (SUM) ^{lú}MAŠ.MAŠ ^{lú}UM.ME.A TIN.TIR^{ki}

1 [... let] me tell you.
2 [This is by Saggil-kīnam-ubbib, contemporary with Adad-apl]a-iddina, the magician, scholar of Babylon.

If Lambert's restoration of this catalogue of ancient texts is correct, this list would also date (E)saggil-kīnam-ubbib to the eleventh century BCE.[37]

Given the lack of conclusive written evidence, however, various modern scholars have challenged the authorship of (E)saggil-kīnam-ubbib and asserted the possibility of pseudepigraphy. For example, D. Sitzler calls (E)saggil-kīnam-

[31] E.g., VAN DIJK 1962, pp. 45 and 51; *RlA* 11, p. 235, Ramman-apla-iddina; FOSTER 2007, p. 34. See also UEHLINGER 2007, p. 147.

[32] See LAMBERT 1962, pp. 64–67; 72–77.

[33] Cf., *RlA* 10, p. 620, Priester §2.4.

[34] For Esagil-kīn-apli, see below.

[35] The names of the kings Nebuchadnezzar I and Adad-apla-iddina appear in reverse order — Nebuchadnezzar died nearly 40 years before Adad-apla-iddina's accession to the throne. Thus, if Esaggil-kīnī-ubba, Esagil-kīnī-ubbalu, and Esagil-kīnam-ubbib are really the same person, he must have served as the main scholar of the Babylonian kings for at least four decades. VAN DIJK 1962, pp. 45 and 51; BRINKMAN 1968, p. 115, note 641; FINKEL 1988, p. 144. In addition, HEEẞEL 2010, p. 164 suggests that Esagil-kīn-apli and Esagil-kīna-ubbib might have been the same person and that he could have written the *Babylonian Theodicy* in his very old age.

[36] LAMBERT 1962, p. 66.

[37] If Lambert's restoration is correct, this would be the only example of a reference to the period during which a particular scholar was active. None of the other entries preserved in the list refer to the kings they served. However, it is also possible that the incipit ... *lu*]-*uq-bi-ka* does not, in fact, refer to the *Babylonian Theodicy* at all and that , ...]-×-SUM is the name of a different scholar from Babylon. Note also VAN DER TOORN 2003, p. 68.

ubbib the "fiktiven Verfasser."[38] Likewise, von Soden, although he does not as such reject (E)saggil-kīnam-ubbib's authorship, argues that the *Babylonian Theodicy* was composed no earlier than *c.* 800 BCE.[39]

Although there is no good reason not to trust the author's 'signature' left in the acrostic,[40] it is problematical to attempt to relate the *Babylonian Theodicy* to any particular historical event as R. Albertz has tried to do.[41] The poem neither alludes to an historical incident nor to a specific personage that might date the text to any particular period. The main topic of the *Babylonian Theodicy* is the importance of worshipping the gods despite occasional sentiments of injustice. The question of theodicy is a ubiquitous and timeless issue, and many people must have been asking the same questions that our protagonist of the *Babylonian Theodicy* has asked here. Likewise, the solution offered by the friend in this text is a very orthodox one within the history of Mesopotamian religion(s). Thus, attempting to relate this text to a particular period hardly contributes to its understanding.

The Story

The *Babylonian Theodicy* evidently forms a dialogue between two learned men, and, as we shall see later, they were probably an *ummânu* and his apprentice.[42] However, we do not find in this composition any of the typical formulae introducing direct speech.[43] Normally, Sumero-Akkadian debating texts begin with a narrative describing the background of the debate, e.g. the identities of the speakers, the place where the conversation took place and so forth.[44] Yet, no such story opens the *Babylonian Theodicy*. Therefore, we know virtually nothing with certainty about the background of the debate. In fact, the very nature of the debate in the *Babylonian Theodicy* is very different from that of other debate texts known to us. Here, unlike the Sumero-Akkadian debate-texts, the speakers make no effort to convince their opponents of their superior authority: instead, the debate concentrates on a point of doctrine, i.e. the meaning of belief in the gods and its benefit.

Although the protagonist is customarily referred to as the 'sufferer', this 'sufferer' of the *Babylonian Theodicy* does not face the kind of physical adversity

[38] SITZLER 1995, p. 101. Note also VAN DER TOORN *ibid.*, p. 69.

[39] VON SODEN 1990, p. 143. See, also LANDSBERGER 1936, p. 36.

[40] JEAN 2006, p. 38.

[41] ALBERTZ 1981 pp. 355–357, 368–369. Note also, VAN DER TOORN 1991, p. 69; *idem* 2003, pp. 75–76. *Contra*, SPIECKERMANN 1998, p. 329, note 2.

[42] See, e.g., VAN DER TOORN 2003, p. 70.

[43] DENNING-BOLLE 1992, pp. 156–157.

[44] For a general discussion of Sumerian dispute-texts, see VANSTIPHOUT 1990; *idem* 1991; *idem* 1992. For a discussion of Akkadian debate-texts, see VOGELZANG 1991. One can compare this practice with the biblical Book of Job, which also begins with an opening narrative and concludes with God's praise of Job.

(e.g. a life-threatening illness). Instead, the he complains that godless fools and impious rascals, whom he tends to envy, amass wealth while the true worshipper of the gods — apparently an allusion to himself — fails to gain material prosperity. Thus he insists that he is a victim of social injustice, and he raises doubts about the meaning of human piety or fairness of the divine-beings. He also claims that he has been persecuted by the wealthy people.[45] On occasion, the sufferer goes so far as to vow to act himself like a robber, to reject the gods, and to abandon his ritual duties, imitating those whom he has called godless fools and impious rascals. Clearly his attitude is a reaction to the belief of the ancient Babylonians that, by demonstrating piety through offerings and prayers, people should gain good health and wealth as rewards.[46]

Although the main text itself does not reveal the exact social status of the protagonist of the poem, most likely he is a scribe. The protagonist's profession becomes particularly evident when one takes into account the *Theodicy Commentary*. In attempting to explain his problem to the friend, the protagonist often uses figurative speech referring to himself as *lāmi iṣṣūrī*, 'bird-catcher,' (line 160) or *usandû*, 'fowler,' (line 202). In the *Theodicy Commentary,* the commentator equates these words with *ṭupšarru*, 'scribe'.[47] Because there is no semantic connection between the terms for 'bird-catcher' or 'fowler' and the term for 'scribe,'[48] it is evident that the intention of these comments is to explain what 'bird-catcher' and 'fowler' really refer to, namely to *THE SCRIBE*, who is the protagonist of the poem.

However, it is hard to believe that the protagonist was just any scribe. Frequently, the friend praises his wisdom with extravagant flattery. For example, lines 56–57:

56 Date palm, tree of wealth, my esteemed brother,
57 sum of all wisdom, jewel of s[agacity],

Another example is line 78:

---

[45] This claim might not be an exaggeration and could well reflect real situations occasionally experienced by *ummânus*. For example, Balasî, the crown prince's *ummânu* who served both Esarhaddon and Assurbanipal, complains of how the chief cupbearer had seized his field and his orchards, apparently without any authorization from the king, SAA 10, no. 58, rev 4–21. A similar incident is reported by Marduk-šumu-uṣur, chief haruspex who also served Esarhaddon and Assurbanipal. In a letter to the king, he charges that the governor of Barhazi had robbed one of his peasants. He further complains about his own poor economic situation, *ibid*., no. 173, obv 6–rev 9. Note also the report sent to Esarhaddon contrasting the house of an un-named chief scribe with that of Aššur-naṣir, a *nobleman*, SAA 16, no. 89. In this letter, the sender of the letter testifies: É LÚ.GAL-A.BA É *qa-lál* [AN]ŠE.NITÁ-*ma ina* ŠÀ-*bi-šú la e-rab* É ^{m}*aš-šur*-PAP-*ir* DUMU.ŠU.SI.MEŠ SIG_5 *bat-qu ma-a*ʾ-*da ina* ŠÀ-*bi*, 'the house of the chief scribe is a tiny house. Even a [do]nkey would not *fit in* (lit.: enter). (Whereas) the house of Aššur-naṣir, a *nobleman*, is beautiful (although) much damaged inside,' (lines 9–15). For the economic problems of the *ummânus* in the Neo-Assyrian period, see LUUKKO 2007, pp. 246–248. Although one may take such incidents to be a sign of the declining power of the Assyrian kings (e.g., PEČÍRKOVÁ 1985, p. 161), it is equally possible that, given such complaints in the *Babylonian Theodicy*, many scholars throughout the entire history of Babylonia may in fact have suffered ill-treatment of this sort by the men of power.

[46] For this, see below.

[47] See, OSHIMA, forthcoming.

[48] It is difficult to believe that these entries refer specifically to the augurs who were also a part of scribal community. For the augurs, particularly in the Neo-Assyrian period, see, RADNER 2009.

78 Righteous one, one who possesses wisdom (lit.: ear), ...

Moreover, the commentaries for lines 6 and 201 in the *Theodicy Commentary* (obv. 3 and rev. 9'), *mu-du-u* = *ṭup-šar-ri*, 'wise, learned = scribe,' suggest that the protagonist is not simply a scribe working as an archivist or administrator but rather a highly educated man who is probably involved in scholarly activities.[49] The repeated references to the obligations to carry out rituals and celebrations suggest his priestly position, namely that of a temple scholar or a royal counsellor, who, like the author himself, normally would have worked very close to the temples.

Similarly, there is no direct indication of the identity of the friend in the *Babylonian Theodicy*. At first, the friend tries to comfort the sufferer and urges him to keep his faith in the gods. Although the friend often replies to the aggressive, often blasphemous, speech of the sufferer with sharp criticism, he generally maintains patience towards him and insists on piety to the gods.[50] The friend repeatedly speaks of the enduring principles of wisdom.[51] Although the friend frequently addresses the sufferer as a wise and learned man, in fact he treats him as a rebellious young man who has not yet attained true wisdom, being like those whom he despises and calls rascals and fools.[52]

An Abstract of the Babylonian Theodicy

Strophe I (Sufferer)
The sufferer complains that his parents died when he was still young and he was left with no guardian.

Strophe II (Friend)
The friend tries to comfort the sufferer with sympathetic words for the death of his parents. He also states that worship of gods brings wealth.

Strophe III (Sufferer)
The sufferer complains about his lack of wealth and vigour.

[49] As ROCHBERG 2000, p. 361 briefly outlines the matter, the term [lú]A.BA = *ṭupšarru*, 'scribe,' was also applied to the specialists on omen texts, or what Rochberg defines as "omen science", — i.e., celestial and terrestrial omen series (*Enūma Anu Enlil*, *Šumma Ālu*, *Šumma Izbu*) and hemerologcial omens (*Iqqur Īpuš* and *Inbu Bēl Arhim*) — with the exception of the extispicy series designated as *bārûtu*. Based on the entry *mu-du-u* = *ṭup-šar-ri* in the *Theodicy Commentary* cited above, one might surmise that the protagonist of the *Babylonian Theodicy* could have been a specialist in "omen science" that also belonged to the fields specialized in by *ummânus* in antiquity. One might further speculate that this entry in the ancient commentary could also be related to the recurrent complaint of the sufferer that he cannot understand the divine *ṭēmu* which could perhaps refer to the omens or signs sent by the gods in addition to the general meanings 'plan, reasoning'. However, because the word *ṭēmu* in the *Babylonian Theodicy* only refers to the divine plan of the society or their wisdom, this interpretation is unlikely. Given the very broad issue of social injustice and unrewarded piety raised in the *Babylonian Theodicy*, I believe that *mūdû* and *ṭupšarru* in this poem refer to the ancient scholars and royal counsellors in general rather than to the specialists in the omen texts.

[50] Cf. STAMM 1944, p. 107.

[51] BOTTÉRO 1977, pp. 30, 35; DENNING-BOLLE 1992, p. 141.

[52] Cf., STAMM 1944, p. 103.

Strophe IV (Friend)
The friend states that prayers and offerings to the gods alone bring divine mercy to people in adversity.

Strophe V (Sufferer)
With metaphors of wild animals (a wild-ass and a lion) — clearly referring to the rich people who do not honour the gods — the sufferer speaks of the injustice in society. He also claims that he is (or has been) always worshipping the gods.

Strophe VI (Friend)
The friend points out that, like the power of the wild animals alluded to by the sufferer in the previous strophe, the riches of the impious are not eternal. Divine blessing alone is everlasting.

Strophe VII (Sufferer)
The sufferer insists that the true worshipers of gods like him become poor whereas the impious amass riches.

Strophe VIII (Friend)
The friend urges the sufferer to continue to observe the rituals although the plans of the gods are difficult to comprehend (and thus the rituals may seem pointless).

Strophes IX–XI are missing.[53]

Strophe XII (Friend)[54]
It seems that the friend describes his devotion to the deities.

Strophe XIII (Sufferer)
The sufferer reaches a breaking point and loses his control. He vows to abandon everything, including his house, his property and the gods' rituals and expresses the desire to become a robber. Clearly the envy of the material riches of the others has corrupted his mind.

Strophe XIV (Friend)
Due to the poor preservation, it is difficult to interpret this section. It seems that the friend criticizes the sufferer for his statements in Strophe XIII.

Strophe XV (Sufferer)
The sufferer bewails the injustice in society and again vows to act as a criminal.

Strophe XVI (Friend)
It seems that the friend begins this speech by addressing the sufferer as a humble man with a healthy mind. However, due to the lacunae, the message of this passage is unclear.

[53] It is very likely that lines 37–40b of the *Theodicy Commentary* are commentaries on words belonging to lines 110–121 of the main text. Given the fact that many entries begin with the syllable *AM*, it is very likely that the entries in *Theodicy Commentary* 37 belong to Strophe XI: ...] ×-*RA*: *a-mur* ('I saw'): *am-mat*: *am-m*[*a-t*]*ú*? ('forearm' or 'strong'): *am-ma-raq* ('I am being scraped, rubbed away'): *ana za-ra-qú* ('to sprinkle'): *am*-×-[: ... Further, see OSHIMA forthcoming.

[54] Strophes XII–XIX are fragmentary. Thus, the summaries for these sections are merely tentative.

Strophe XVII (Sufferer)
It seems that the sufferer speaks of people who once were rich but then lost their property and now lack food, i.e. the barest necessities.

Strophe XVIII (Friend)
It seems that the friend insists that devotion to gods ultimately decides who will be rich or poor.

Strophe XIX (Sufferer)
It seems that the sufferer presents himself as a well-educated scribe who lacks sufficient means.

Strophe XX (Friend)
The friend claims that devotion to gods will eventually reward people with blessing and urges the sufferer to maintain the rituals.

Strophe XXI (Sufferer)
In an aggressive tone, the sufferer replies to the friend's appeal to honour the gods. He later bemoans his poverty.

Strophe XXII (Friend)
The friend maintains his position that the wealth of a fool who does not honour the gods will not last forever and that only those who trust in the gods will eventually be rewarded.

Strophe XXIII (Sufferer)
The sufferer also maintains his position and speaks of the unfairness of society.

Strophe XXIV (Friend)
The friend agrees that there is certain unfairness in the world that is determined by the divine plan; he insists, however, that a human being cannot comprehend the gods' decision.

Strophe XXV (Sufferer)
The sufferer opens this speech without praising the friend's wisdom, but instead passionately appealing to be listened to. He again repeats his thesis that an evil person lives long and well, while a *pitiable*[55] but pious person is persecuted by the rich.

Strophe XXVI (Friend)
After a long discourse, the friend finally accepts the argument of the sufferer — though only partially — and he concedes that there is a certain injustice in society. He explains that this originates from the lies and falsity that the great gods gave to mankind upon its creation. However, he does not forget to use this in order to make a point of his own thesis: People persecute the *pitiable* because he has no divine guidance.

Strophe XXVII (Sufferer)
Unlike the typical ending of other Mesopotamian discourse texts, in the *Babylonian Theodicy*, there is no concluding praise of 'the winner' by a god. Having

[55] This word *dunnamû* is normally translated 'a man of low-status, a fool.' For my translation, 'a pitiable, pitiful (person),' see pp. xxx–xxxi below.

heard the last friend's last speech, the sufferer suddenly gives up the aggressive and defensive tone of his speech and turns to the friend with humble appeals for help. He even turns to the gods with a *cri de cœur* for his salvation. The poem ends, then, with a plea to the human king to lead humankind to the way of the gods.

The Message of the *Babylonian Theodicy*

To grasp the intention of the *Babylonian Theodicy*, one must note the connections between the following points:

I: The friend's repeated insistence on three points: (A) mankind has no ability to understand the divine will or plans; (B) the wealth of the godless does not last long; (C) one should seek the blessing of the gods by means of piety (rituals, prayers, offerings).

II: The last argument of the sufferer and the friend's response (Strophes XXV–XXVI)

III: The prayer of the sufferer (Strophe XXVII)

In what follows, I will discuss each of these points in turn.

I: *The three major points repeatedly made by the friend*

As different modern scholars have already noted,[56] throughout the text, the friend reiterates the same three theses, using different words to do so:

A) the incomprehensible character of the divine will/plan (82–83; 256–264);
B) the impermanent wealth of the faithless (59–65; 188–198; 235–238);
C) the importance of rituals as the means to attaining the divine realm of blessing (19–22; 39–44; 66; 79–81; 84–88; 212–220; 239–242).

These theses are set forth as replies to the sufferer's doubts about divine and social justice.

For example, in lines 48–51, the sufferer had used the metaphors of the onager and the lion in order to describe the opulence of the faithless ones:

48 Has the wild-ass, the onager, which was sated with e[ars of barley],
49 paid attention to the one who guarantees me divine wisdom?
50 Has the savage lion who always ate the *best* meat,
51 (ever) brought *maḫṣatu*-flour-offering [in order to] appease [a furio]us god?

Replying in lines 59–64, the friend says:

59 (But), i[n the steppe], look at the *perfect* (*animal*) of the steppe, the onager:
60 the arrow will bring down the one who trampled all the (cultivated) meadowland.

[56] E.g., BOTTÉRO 1977, pp. 30, 35; DENNING-BOLLE 1992, p. 141.

61 Come, *think about* (lit.: look carefully at) the lion, the attacker of livestock, which you mentioned (earlier),
62 (for) the crime which the lion committed, a pit opened up for it.
63 The one who is assigned wealth, the rich man who piled up treasures,
64 like the Fire-God, the ruler will burn (him) before his time.

The message of the friend is clear: Just as the strong wild-ass and the mighty lion will perish for their crimes, so will the rich be consumed by fire for their unseemly wealth. On the other hand, in lines 65–66 which follow, the friend asserts, that riches received as a reward of piety will be everlasting:

65 Do you wish to go the way these (people/things) have gone?
66 Always seek the ever-lasting *blessing of favour* of the divine-being.

As in this section (Strophe V), the friend combines the points (A) and (C) in his answer, for example in lines 235–242 (Strophe XXII):

235 As for the rogue whose prosperity you desired,
236 the *agility*? of his leg will be soon lost,
237 The villain who has no god may gain possession,
238 (but) a killer with his weapon pursues him.
239 If you do not seek the *will* of the god, what is your gain?
240 The one who bears the yoke of the god is indeed thin but his meal is regularly (*served*).
241 Seek constantly after the pleasant wind of (the) gods,
242 you shall regain at once what you have lost at the harvest time.

Unfortunately the sufferer's speech in the previous strophe (XXI) has too many lacunae to recover its message. Yet, given the patterns repeated in the poem, very likely the sufferer here expressed his intention to abandon his faith and to gain riches just like the godless rogues he despises.

In response, the friend repeatedly asserts that mankind cannot comprehend the divine plan and that no one can explain the rationality behind it, e.g., lines 256–264:

256 The *divine* mind is as far as the centre of the heavens,
257 *comprehending it* is very difficult; people cannot understand.
258 The creation of the hand of Aruru, altogether *living-creatures*,
259 why do the *human beings*, all of them, not *pay attention*.
260 The first calf of a cow is inferior
261 a later scion will *be* doubly *good as* it.
262 The first son is born a fool,
263 (but) this second (son)'s reputation is capable and heroic.
264 Although one might be attentive, people cannot understand what the *divine plan* (could) be.

Despite the friend's admission of the unfair and inequality distribution of physical strength and intelligence among people, a basic sense of trust in the divine plan pervades his speech. His argument seems to be that, although it might seem unjust that the gods designed such inequalities, there must be a good reason for them.

Thus, he argues, despite the apparent unfairness of the gods' decisions, the world is not as hopeless as the sufferer claims it to be. The friend asserts that, although we cannot comprehend the gods' minds (*ṭēmu*), we can still gain divine blessings by practicing the rituals, lines 82–84:

82 Like the centre of the heavens, the plans of (the) gods are dis[tant],
83 the command of (a) god and (a) goddess is not hea[rd],
84 (but) human beings are *well* acquainted with rituals.

These counsels given by the friend are not new and similar ideas have frequently been formulated by various Sumero-Akkadian thinkers. For example, the benefits of piety to the gods are well expressed in a bilingual proverb known from first millennium Assyria, the *Assyrian Collection*, ii 23–26 (LAMBERT 1960, p. 227):

23 When you *think* (of your god),
24 your god is yours.
25 When you do not *think* (of your god),
26 your god is not yours.

As Lambert notes, the sentence 'your god is yours' probably corresponds to "the same idea as 'having a god', i.e. being successful."[57]

This belief that piety brings wealth was in fact very old, and an allusion to such a notion is attested as early as the early second millennium. For example, the *Instructions of Ur-Ninurta* explains the connection between piety and welfare as a divine favour, while it also warns against the misfortunes of the impious; see lines 19–37:[58]

19 A man who knows how to respect the affairs of the gods (i.e., worship),
20 who fulfils the offerings to the gods,
21 who ...... (and) offers sacrifice,
22 to whom the name of his god is precious
23 who stays away from maliciousness and curse,
24 who goes straight to the place of gods,
25 what he has lost will be restored to him
26 days will be added to his *life* (lit.: days),
27 years will be plenty in addition to the years he (already) has,
28 his descendants will experience good health

---

[57] LAMBERT 1960, p. 231. See also, JACOBSEN 1976, pp. 155–156. Incidentally, for the interpretation of *kapādu*, as normally meaning 'to plan,' see Lambert's note on *op. cit.*

This notion that a man together with his god is successful whereas a man without his god does not succeed is already frequently expressed in Sumerian proverbs. For example, UET 6/2, 251 (= ALSTER 1997, p. 309):

A man without a (personal) god
does not gain much food, does not gain (even) a little food,
going out to a river, he does not catch a fish.
Going out to a field, he does not catch a gazelle.
He *can*not match (his) great opponents.
When running, he does not reach (his goal).
(Yet,) if his god becomes favourable towards him,
anything that he names will be provided for him.

[58] ALSTER 2005, pp. 228–231. For further discussions related to the *Instructions of Ur-Ninurta* that also deal with the possible purpose, the dating and the origin of that text, see *ibid.*, pp. 221–224. See also UEHLINGER 2007, pp. 125–127, esp. 127.

29 his heir will pour water libations for him.
29a [His] god will look favourably upon him,
29b [he (his god) will] listen to *his prayer* (lit.: him) and he (i.e., the man) will be prosper,
29c he will *look after* him (lit.: stare).
30 But the man who does not observe the affairs of the gods (i.e., worship),
30a who does not fulfil the offerings to the gods,
31 to whom prayers are not (held) dear,
32 to whom maliciousness and curse are not abominable
32a to whom the name of his god is not precious,
33 the days when he lives will not be prosperous,
34 his descendants will not experience good health,
35 his heir will not pour water libations for him,
35a his descendants will not experience long lasting health.
36 Has a man who does not respect his god *ever gained wealth* or *seen success*?
37 These are instructions of the gods.

This idea that a god will reward the piety of his wards with riches is not limited to the ancient pragmatic and didactic texts but also attested in religious texts. The desire for wealth as a reward for piety is attested not only in canonical prayers but also in private supplications. For example, a prayer engraved on a Kassite cylinder seal offers the following plea, LAMBERT 1970, p. 46:[59]

May (whatever) I have desired be (my) gain,
may (whatever) I sought be (my) favour.
The petitions to Marduk
and to Zarpanītu
I have offered. Let me see favour.
The seal of Šumuḫ-Nergal.

As becomes clear from these examples, in the *Babylonian Theodicy*, the friend teaches nothing other than the orthodox doctrines that had already been established by the early second millennium and were still maintained even in the first millennium. In short, the friend should be understood as the personification of those principles that had been sustained by the Mesopotamian thinkers over at least one thousand years.[60]

II: *The Last Argument of the Sufferer and the Friend's Response* (*Strophes XXV–XXVI*)

In Strophe XXV, the sufferer argues that people honour rich and powerful persons who are wicked, while they mistreat the poor and the helpless, although righteous persons, who respect the gods. The sufferer's last phrase in this stanza, "and as for me, the weak one, a rich man *keeps* persecuting me," makes clear the protago-

---

[59] = LIMET 1971, 9.4.

[60] Cf., BUCCELLATI 1972, p. 171. Note also MATTINGLY 1990, p. 325: "the scribe from Nippur who wrote [Sumerian] *Man and His God* would have been most comfortable with the poem written by Saggil-kinam-ubbib many centuries later."

nist's position — he is clearly speaking of himself when he refers to the *pitiable*, innocuous, righteous, pious, helpless, and powerless person. He insists that he is the victim of social injustice and that the gods have failed him.

Modern scholars have assumed that in the following stanza (XXVI), the friend comes to agree with the sufferer that there is indeed a certain injustice in human society. The friend even identifies the source of such injustice, as being the lies and unjustness given to mankind by the gods, lines 276–280:

276 The king of the pre-eminent (ones) (i.e., gods) Narru (=Enlil), the creator the people,
277 the noble Zulummaru (=Ea), the one who pinched off their clay,
278 the queen, the one who shapes them, the mistress Mami,
279 gave *twisted* speech to humankind:
280 They (also) bestowed upon them (i.e., mankind) lies and *falsehood* for all time.

With these phrases, the friend explains that lies, falsity, deceit and unjustness are part of human nature. The ancient Mesopotamians believed that personal gods are responsible for teaching men ethics and morals. That means that the pious person bears no sins, because his personal gods are with him and give him divine instructions about justice. In addition, the ancients apparently believed that the personal gods also 'corrected' the speech of their protégés. For example, a lengthy Akkadian prayer to Marduk, states, *Prayer to Marduk no. 1*, lines 111–113,[61] states:

111 When you (Marduk), his god, are at his (the protégé's) side,
112 his speech is well chosen, his word is honest.
113$^{?}$ his mouth$^{?}$ does not bear crime […

These lines from the prayer to Marduk suggest that gods not only teach man how to behave morally and ethically, but also how to speak correctly. Based on this, one can speculate that the ancients did not believe that we human beings could act according to the divine ethics and morals without divine guidance.

The following four lines (283–287) of the *Babylonian Theodicy* are normally taken to refer to the fate of the righteous poor with an allusion to the protagonist. Until now, this interpretation of the *Babylonian Theodicy* has not been challenged because it was routinely assumed that Strophe XXVI is a speech of the friend sympathizing with the sufferer. However, this assumption causes a number of difficulties for understanding the poem as a whole, in particular with regard to Strophe XXVII, which is the sufferer's concluding speech. Later we shall come back to these lines (283–287) but first we need to discuss Strophe XXVII as a whole, in order to clarify the problems raised by the traditional interpretation.

III: *The Prayer of the Sufferer* (*Strophe XXVII*)

Although the *Babylonian Theodicy* is a poem in dialogue form, Strophe XXVII follows a classical formula found in Akkadian prayers, namely: an opening invocation, followed by the suppliant's lament, his self-identification, and finally his pleas. Initially, the protagonist appears to argue that he has experienced unmerited

[61] Oshima 2011, pp. 164–165.

dismay despite his righteousness, but then the tone of his voice suddenly becomes very humble and, at the end, he turns to the gods and the king to beg for his salvation. Modern scholars have been puzzled by this apparent sudden change in the sufferer's attitude,[62] shifting from his boasting speech in Strophe XXV to the humble prayer in Strophe XXVII — and have offered different interpretations. However, no consensus has yet been reached.

First we examine the opening phrases of this strophe, 287–288:

287 O my friend, you are merciful: Examine (my) grief,
288 help me: I have seen hardships, you shall know.

The first phrase is generally interpreted as an acknowledgment of the friend's kindness in accepting the situation of the protagonist. For example VON SODEN 1990, p. 145 interprets the last Strophe as follows:

> "Die letzte Erwiderung des Freundes in Strophe XXVI gibt dem Dulder Recht und nennt darüber hinaus die Götter, die Unwahrhaftigkeit und die Lust zu ungerechtem Handeln »geschenkt« hätten. Jede Überheblichkeit ist ihm vergangen; er wagt keine Mahnung mehr. Eben dadurch macht er [i.e. the friend] das Schlußwort des Dulders in Strophe XXVII möglich, das zunächst seine [i.e. the friend's] Barmherzigkeit dankbar anerkennt, sich dann vor Gott und Göttin demütigt, auf jede weitere Klage verzichtet und, ohne die direkte Anrede an die Gottheit zu wagen, Hilfe und Erbarmen erbittet."

H. Spieckermann also sees this line to refer to the friend's "Tat der Barmherzigkeit" toward the sufferer.[63]

W. G. Lambert likewise interprets this text as indicating that the friend in the end has accepted the sufferer's position by telling the story of the creation of humankind and institution of deceitful nature. LAMBERT 1995 pp. 35–36:

> "Powerful but wicked men, he [i.e. the sufferer] argues, constantly oppress the pious poor. This time the friend fully accepts the point and goes on to explain it: that the human race has a perverse streak because the gods created them this way: 'With lies, and not truth, they endowed them for ever.' So it is, he continues, that the rich and powerful grind down poor. So agreement has at last been reached, and by implication the sufferer has gone though his life of misery because the gods implanted a criminal bent in the human race at the time of creation. ... That lying should have been given to the human race as an enjoined norm is not surprising when the gods themselves in myths also lied. ... Thus the doctrine of the Theodicy was in no way original; the originality, so far as our knowledge extends, was its use of this old teaching in a context where its mention implicitly cast doubts on whether the gods do maintain justice in the universe, and so on the point previously upheld in this text, namely that piety pays. Though the relevance of this old doctrine is not made explicit, it seems clear that the author meant the point to be taken, because it is the one point accepted without reservation by the friend, and once it has been asserted and accepted by both disputants, there is no further discussion."[64]

---

[62] E.g., BOTTÉRO 1977, pp. 41–42.

[63] SPIECKERMANN 1998, p. 340.

[64] Note also, LAMBERT 1960, p 65. For similar suggestions, see, e.g., VAN DER TOORN 1991, p. 70.

As Lambert and other modern scholars rightly suggest, the author of the *Babylonian Theodicy* evidently relates social injustice to the lies and deceit of mankind that had been 'implanted' in human beings by the gods as part of their nature. But that is only one part of the complicated lesson that the *Babylonian Theodicy* offers. Lambert's interpretation does not, in fact, offer any convincing explanation for the sudden change of the sufferer's voice in Strophe XXVII.[65]

SITZLER 1995, p. 108 and note 428 suggests that the friend probably acts as a defender of the divine order in Strophe XXVI. She further speculates that the last speech of the sufferer was an attempt to please the friend.[66] In addition, she offers the following interpretation in order to explain the sufferer's petition for help:[67]

> "Für den Gerechten gibt es keinen Gewinn, d.h. keinen angemessenen Platz in der Gesellschaft mehr, aber er kann aufgrund seiner Gerechtigkeit auf die Hilfe der Gottheit und des Königs hoffen. Der Text der Babylonischer Theodizee endet so im Umschwung der Anklage zur Klage mit dem Ziel der Hilfe. Damit verbunden ist eine Veränderung des Welt- und des Gottesbildes von der Vorstellung der Ordnungsmächte zur Vorstellung der persönlichen Frömmighkeit. Die Alternative wäre die Abkehr von allen Werten und Göttern, wie sie in der Dichtung vom Kläger eingebracht wird. Die Aufgabe der Dichtung ist es nun, den Weisen in ähnlicher Situation auch zum Wandel des Welt- und Gottesbildes und nicht zur Abkehr von den Göttern zu leiten. Die Vorwürfe nehmen dabei die Argumente der Leser auf und machen den Kläger als ihren typischen Vertreter glaubwürdig."

However, if one pays close attention to the mid-section of the poem, one notices that the sufferer is not nearly as righteous as he claims to be. Thus, in the Strophes XIII, XV and XVII, he vows to act as a robber or at least to abandon the religious duties. Such statements are nothing less than a challenge to the very foundations of the divine and social orders and, therefore, would have been regarded blasphemous. He clearly declares his intention to act exactly like those whom he had called rascals and rogues. In fact, the friend repeatedly criticizes such an impious attitude on the part of the sufferer, for example lines 212–214:

212 You make your clever mind *go* (lit.: have) astray
213 […] . wisdom you drove away
214 [you (have) scorned] (divine) guidance and slandered (divine) laws.

Another example is line 255:

255 (because) your heart is angered, you *turn to* god with disrespect.

Obviously, the riches of other people and their greed have corrupted the sufferer's faith and engendered a criminal mind in him. Thus, he can hardly be called a "Gerechter".[68]

---

[65] Note also, POPE 1974, p. LXVII: "The ending of the Babylonian Theodicy is very strange. … no real effort is made to solve the problem. The final admission of the friend that men are sinful because the gods made them so, is a part of the actual problem and contributes nothing to the solution."

[66] SITZLER 1995, p. 108.

[67] *Ibid.*, p. 109. Cf. also UEHLINGER 2007, p. 156.

[68] Note UEHLINGER 2007, pp. 157–158, note 179: "Anders als in den zuvor behandelten Dichtungen [namely the Sumerian *Man and his God*, the Babylonian *Man and his God*, *Marduk Praise from Ugarit* (*Ugaritica* 5, no. 162) and *Ludlul Bēl Nēmeqi*] ist der Klagende der *Theodizee*

Sitzler's argument, in fact, contains a serious misunderstanding of the concept of guilt among the ancient Mesopotamians. Turning our attention to the last three lines of the poem, lines 295–297, we read the following petitions:

295 May (the) gods, who *have has forsaken* me, establish help (for me).
296 May (the) goddess who d[eserted me] have mercy on me.
297 May the shepherd, my Sun, gui[de back] the people to the god.

In this section, the sufferer clearly states that he has been abandoned by the gods. The ancients attributed the abandonment of people by the gods to the deities' dissatisfaction with the people abandoned, mostly because of their sins and lack of piety. In other words, when someone appeals for mercy and salvation from the gods who have abandoned him, he simultaneously admits his guilt, i.e., either his sins against the divine or at least his lack of piety towards them. Thus, the last lines in the *Babylonian Theodicy* are not mere expressions of the sufferer's piety to the gods, but rather they are pleas for their forgiveness and reconciliation with him. No truly righteous person would need to make such a request and admit his sins against the gods.

DENNING-BOLLE 1992, p. 150, on the other hand, takes the sufferer's last speech to be "the final apology" to his friend and the gods. She also concludes:

> "In these last three lines [i.e. lines 295–297] of the dialogue, we seem to witness the sufferer's ultimate declaration of trust in the Divine. This is, indeed, what the friend has been stressing for the entire discussion. It would appear, then, that the sufferer has agreed with the friend and he affirms his trust in the eternal agency of the gods."[69]

She further states that the sufferer has now come around to accepting the friend's position "by confirming his ultimate confidence" in the gods at the same time that the friend comes to a certain agreement with the sufferer.[70] Yet, her interpretation does not explain why the sufferer should conclude his acceptance with an appeal for recognition of his suffering (lines 287–288). She appears to have failed to realize the significance of line 287. The sentence "O my friend, you are merciful: Examine (my) grieving" is not a profession of gratitude but rather an invocation and a cry for help.

Addressing someone as 'merciful' does not always serve as an acknowledgement of the kindness and leniency of the one addressed. In the Akkadian prayers, for example, the supplicants very often address the gods as 'merciful' and praise their capability to redeem people while extolling at the same time the gods' anger and devastating powers in an attempt to seek reconciliation with them. This

nicht nur kein Gerechter, sondern offensichtlich auch kein Formmer mehr: Hier geschieht eine Weichenstellung, die dem Szenario der Hiob-Dichtung (nicht der Rahmenerzählung!) vorausliegt und dieses vielleicht überhaupt ermöglicht hat."

BUCCELLATI 1981, p. 37 speculates that "the Theodicy includes a specific call to reject established religion." Note also, BUCCELLATI 1972, pp .173–175. One might also speculate that the author intended to evoke a rejection of ritual oriented religion. However, as MATTINGLY 1990, p. 327, replies, Buccellati's "suggestion is too modern and not in keeping with the sufferer's acquiescence in the poem's conclusion." By the same token, the message given in the acrostic likewise gives no support to such speculations.

[69] DENNING-BOLLE 1992, p. 151.

[70] *Ibid*. BUCCELLATI 1972, p. 173 suggests that the sufferer and the friend reached complete agreement and became "*noi*" (we).

sounds very enigmatic but it is very common in the Akkadian prayer genre.[71] For example, a *Šuila*-prayer to Marduk, BMS 12, line 40:[72]

40 *re-mé-na-ta* EN *ina* PAP.ḪAL *u* KI.KAL *tu-še-zeb en-ši*
40 You (Marduk) are merciful, Lord, in difficulties and dismay, you save the weak.

This is not simply an acknowledgment of Marduk's kindness, but is rather an invocation of the particular feature of the deity that the supplicant appeals to for his purpose, i.e., reconciliation with Marduk and cure from his illness.[73] Thus, as in the case of BMS 12, we should interpret the first phrase of line 287 of the *Babylonian Theodicy* as being not an acknowledgement of the friend's kindness but rather an appeal for mercy. But why, then, should the sufferer suddenly address the friend with an appeal for mercy? The key to solving this question is found in the interpretation of lines 283–286, in particular, *dunnamû* in line 283. Thus, we must turn our attention back to Strophe XXVI.

The word *dunnamû* in line 283 was intentionally used with an allusion to the protagonist reflecting the use of the same word in line 268 above. It seems that Ebeling's "der Schwächling" and "die schwachen Menschen"[74] as well as Landsberger's "die Armseligen" and "die armseligen Menschen"[75] gained canonical status as the translation of the *dunnamû* in these lines from the *Babylonian Theodicy* and it is routinely translated almost identically by different modern scholars: e.g., "powerless," "a poor man,"[76] "le pauvre,"[77] "den Schwachen," and "den schwächlichen Mann."[78] Therefore, Strophe XXVI is normally taken to be a sympathizing speech delivered by the friend. However, as indicated by ancient synonym lists, the word *dunnamû* not only means 'poor' or 'weak' but also 'a fool'. For example, *Malku* = *Šarru* IV 47–48 equates *dunnamû* with *enšu*, 'weak,' and *ulālu*, 'fool.'[79] When we now read the last four lines of Strophe XXVI (283–286) with the latter sense in mind, this passage gains a rather different tone. Thus, departing from the customary interpretation, I propose '*pitiable* (*person*)' as a translation of *dunnamû* in order to convey simultaneously the two different meanings of the word:

283 People treat the *pitiable* (*man*) badly like a thief.
284 They *behave towards* him *maliciously*; they plan his murder.
285 Falsely all the bad things were taught to him because he has no guidance.
286 They will make him fall down like a powerless (man); they will extinguish him like glowing ashes.

---

71 OSHIMA 2011, p. 50.
72 MAYER 1993, p. 317; OSHIMA, *op. cit.*, pp. 356–357, line 24.
73 BMS 12, lines 75–80.
74 EBELING 1924, pp. 15–16, lines 246 and 261.
75 LANDSBERGER 1936, pp. 69 and 71, lines 268 and 283.
76 LAMBERT 1960, pp. 87, 89; FOSTER 2005, pp. 920–921; *CAD* Š/2, p. 48, *šarāku* A, 3 c).
77 LABAT 1970, pp. 326–327.
78 VON SODEN 1990, pp. 156–157.
79 HRŮŠA 2010, pp. 94–95.

Unlike the translations offered previously by the different scholars, this reading of the friend's speech no longer sounds sympathetic, but is, in fact, condemnatory instead. In the previous section (lines 276–280), the friend had accepted the position of the sufferer and explained that social injustice was a result of the deceitful human nature established by the gods. But, for him, their responsibility is limited to the creation of mankind and the institution of lies and falsity as a basic human character.[80] Thus, in the last four lines of this strophe, the friend declares that the protagonist, described here as the *pitiable one*, meets his terrible fate at the hands of people precisely because he lacks divine guidance; in short, the friend insists that the protagonist's sufferings are his own fault, i.e. the result of his repeated blasphemous utterances against the divine order and his lack of respect for the gods as expressed repeatedly in the discourse. He has not, in fact, been as pious as he claims to have been in the previous portions of the text.

In view of the fact discussed above that the author has marked out these four lines from the rest of the strophe by means of rhymes more closely arranged than elsewhere in this strophe and that the last line is the 'odd line' of this stanza, it is almost certain that this passage contains the main message of Strophe XXVI. It is not at all an expression of sympathy, but rather an expression of his angry condemnation of the protagonist's foolishness and a declaration of the terrible fate awaiting him. This interpretation alone can explain why, in the following section, the sufferer turns to the friend with an invocation seeking his mercy and an appeal to re-examine his suffering.

At the beginning of Strophe XVII, the sufferer of the *Babylonian Theodicy* does not accept the friend's accusation that he is a fool or that he has altogether failed to grasp the message of the friend's speech. Thus, in line 289, the sufferer still describes himself as a wise and pious man:

289 I am the *talented* one, ever praying.

In the next line, line 290, however, in spite of this claim, it seems that the sufferer begins to realize the painful reality that he has now been left alone without any help:

290 I found neither help nor aids at the moment.

And in the following section, the sufferer goes on to describe his despair at not finding help, lines 291–294:

291 I shall *tread* the *plaza* of my city quietly,
292 the outcry (has) not became loud; my *voice* (has) been lowered.
293 I do not lift up my head high, I star[e] at the ground.
294 I do not praise the (assembly)-*mem*[*bers*] in the assembly like a slave.

These statements of the sufferer are rather peculiar.

In Akkadian prayers, after the requests for forgiveness, for removal of sins, and for redemption in their adversities, the supplicants often offer pleas to be al-

[80] For this subject, see below.

lowed to enter public places, like the market places and city squares. For example, a prayer to Ištar lines 83–84 (*STC* II, pl. LXXXII and duplicates):[81]

83 Break my manacles, institute my freedom,
84 set my step(s) straight, cheerfully and *proudly* (literally, in princely fashion), let me walk on the street with the living people.

The main purpose of such a 'pilgrimage' was probably to allow the redeemed person to tell about his being saved by the gods and to allow people to witness the saving deeds of the gods.[82] For example, the reciter of a lengthy prayer to Marduk offers the following plea to Marduk, *Prayer to Marduk no. 1*, lines 181–188:[83]

181 May everyone who sees him in the street praise your divinity,
may they say: "(Only) the lord can revive the dead."
May everyone who sees him in the street praise your divinity,
may they say: "(Only) Marduk [c]an revi[ve] the dead."
185 And the servant whose life you spared [*in*? *his difficulty*?],
to the whole people, let him [pro]claim your greatness.
[L]et him praise the one who showed him the light in hi[s] *grave* (lit.: death),
let him bless you continuously […] .. with him.

By contrast, the 'pilgrimage' of the sufferer of the *Babylonian Theodicy* is not a cheerful one at all, but quite the opposite — the picture that he describes is that of someone stricken without hope of help.

In addition, while 'to keep the head down' could be rendered 'to be humiliated, to be depressed,' in Akkadian texts, the expression 'to raise the head' means not only 'to be/make someone proud of' or 'to heed someone,' i.e. listen to or notice them, but also 'to save someone' or 'to be saved'. For example, a poem of praise to Marduk found in Ugarit, *Ugaritica* 5, no. 162, states as follows, lines 13–14:[84]

13' Until the lord raised my head,[85]
14' (when) he revived the dead man — me,

Given this interpretation, it is very likely that lines 291–294 of the *Babylonian Theodicy* describe the sufferer's despair upon realizing that he no longer has any help. It would appear that the friend has given up on him and has left the discourse.

Thus, in the end, despite his occasional threats during the discourse with the friend to abandon the cultic duties, the sufferer is forced to turn to the gods for his salvation, not because he finds himself entitled to do so by reason of his righteousness but because he realizes that, now, the friend has abandoned him, he has no one to guide him to the path of the true belief in the gods. The sufferer begs the

---

[81] For an edition of this *Šuila*-prayer to Ištar with a full *Partitur* with other manuscripts, see Zgoll 2003, pp. 41–67.

[82] Cf., Mayer 1976, pp. 327–328.

[83] Oshima 2011, pp. 168–169.

[84] Oshima, *ibid*., pp. 208–209.

[85] Note also a plea in *Prayer to Marduk no. 1* line 175: *ul-li re-ši-šú šu-lum i-bi-šum*, 'Raise up his (the sufferer's) head; proclaim well-being for him', Oshima, *op. cit*., pp. 168–169.

gods, who have abandoned him, for leniency and help and he petitions the king to lead people to the gods.

As discussed above, by offering his appeals to the gods to be reconciled with them, the protagonist effectively admits his guilt, because the ancient Mesopotamians normally perceived abandonment by the gods to be the outcome of their sins (including, of course, lack of piety). Put differently — the sufferer has finally realized that he has suffered maltreatment from others, not because of any lack of divine justice but because of his own lack of respect for the divine order and his own lack of piety to the gods. This interpretation coincides well with the friend's accusation in line 285 that the protagonist (alias *dunnamû*, 'the pitiable one') is undergoing all the evil falsehoods because of his lack of divine guidance. Thus, despite his protestations in the first half of Strophe XXVII, the protagonist finally comes to accept the friend's accusations and humbly turns back to the gods.

The *Babylonian Theodicy* concludes with an appeal to the human king for the (re)-establishment of piety to the gods. Until now, modern scholars have speculated that the last sentence of the *Babylonian Theodicy* is either a request for the gods' blessing on the sufferer (LANDSBERGER 1936, p. 73; LABAT 1970, p. 327; VON SODEN 1990, p. 157) or a statement that the Sun-god Šamaš guides people like a god (LAMBERT 1960, p. 89; FOSTER 2005, p. 922). However, based on the *Babylonian Theodicy Commentary*, it is now clear that the last word of line 297 should be restored *li-saḫ-ḫ*[*ir*][86] instead of Lambert's *ir*-[ʾ-*e*], "(For the shepherd Šamaš) guides,"[87] or von Soden's *sa*-[*li-mu lid-din*], "möge wie ein Gott Ver[söhnung schenken]."[88] The protagonist is asking the king to help people (re)-gain faith in the gods in the hope of re-establishing the divine order and blessings. Just like the acrostic of this poem, this lengthy ancient literary text concludes with a profession of faith in the gods and the king.

The Source of the Adversity

As already stated above in the discussion of the sufferer's maltreatment by people, the *Babylonian Theodicy* explains that the great gods (Enlil, Ea, and the Mother-Goddess) had bestowed perverse talk and falsity upon mankind when they created them (lines 276–279).

LAMBERT 1995, p. 36 has noted that "[t]hat lying should have been given to the human race as an enjoined norm is not surprising when the gods themselves in myths also lied." He also refers to *lul-da*, 'lying,' among the lists of divine *mes*.[89] He takes this quality of the gods and mankind as the true ground of adversity.[90]

But it seems that the author of the *Babylonian Theodicy* implies that the gods' responsibility is limited only to the creation of mankind with the institution of lies

[86] OSHIMA, forthcoming.

[87] LAMBERT 1960, p. 88.

[88] VON SODEN 1990, p. 157, note 297 b).

[89] LAMBERT 1995, p. 36.

[90] Cf., also, VON SODEN 1990, p. 145.

and falsity being part of mankind's basic character, because he blames the sufferer's lack of divine guidance as being the true reason for his plight (283–295). Thus, one may, also speculate that, with the constitution of falsity and deception as the basic nature of humankind, the author, Saggil-kīnam-ubbib, actually identifies the reason why people do not follow the divine laws and the human king as the protector of the divine order. In fact, the sufferer himself, in line 270, states that he is "a righteous person (*kīnu*) who pays attention" to the divine plan/order (*ṭēmu*), i.e., the religious obligations. With this statement, the sufferer effectively claims that performing rituals is the essence of the divine ethics. In other words, for the ancient Babylonian thinkers, 'to be righteous' meant 'to fulfil religious obligations.'

If my interpretation of the *Babylonian Theodicy* is correct, these passages well parallel the situation of the narrator of *Ludlul Bēl Nēmeqi*,[91] Šubši-mešrê-Šakkan, in Tablet I. He states that, when Marduk had decided to punish him, i.e. the narrator (*Ludlul* I 41–42) — apparently because of his negligence towards the cult of Marduk,[92] he first lost his personal gods and protective spirits (*Ludlul* I 43–46). After his personal gods and protective spirits had forsaken him, his omens and signs became confused and people started saying malicious things about him. He then states that "the king, the flesh of gods, the sun of his people," became furious, while the courtiers planned evil against him (*Ludlul* I 47–72). Unlike the *Babylonian Theodicy*, *Ludlul Bēl Nēmeqi* offers no explanation of why people possess the 'dark side.' For example, the king became furious about the narrator not because he was evil or because the king had something against him personally but rather because Marduk had decided to punish him. That is to say, even the king is no more than a tool of the divine punishment regardless of his nature. One is also reminded of the seven people planning evil actions against the narrator in *Ludlul* I 59–64. They act just like the normal evil demons that are frequently said to be sent by the gods to bring punishment to people that deserve it.

As far as the ancient thinkers are concerned, the evil demons were divine beings and some of them were even honoured as the children or messengers of the prominent gods.[93] For example, Lamaštu, the demoness most feared by the ancients for her vicious devastating power,[94] was the daughter of Anu,[95] just like the mother-goddess Mami,[96] or the goddess of war and sex Ištar[97]. Unlike Judeo-

---

[91] For a recent edition of *Ludlul Bēl Nēmeqi*, see, ANNUS and LENZI 2010.

[92] LAMBERT 1960, p. 56, line p.

[93] Given the neutral nature of these beings, CUNNINGHAM 2007, p. 39, for example, offers the term "*daimon*" in order to refer to them. Note also his observation that "they are divine agents capable of helping as well as harming rather than diabolic forces opposed to the senior deities," *ibid*.

[94] FARBER 2007.

[95] *RlA* 6, p. 439, Lamaštu § 1.

[96] E.g., the Old Babylonian hymn to Mama in the Jena tablet collection (HS 1884), rev i 9', (KREBERNIK 2003/4, p. 16):

9 Mama, the first-born of Anu, the one who sits in the holy Keš.

For Enki or Enlil being the father the Mother-Goddess, see *RlA* 8, p. 507, Muttergöttin A. I., § 4.1.

[97] E.g., *Gilgameš Epic*, Tablet VI, 80–82 (GEORGE 2003, pp. 622–263):

80 When Ištar heard this (the insults from Gilgameš)

Christian beliefs, no known ancient texts state that these evil demons were created in order to bring misery and sorrow to the righteous or to slander and corrupt people like Satan in the Old Testament, Rabbinic Judaism and the New Testament.[98] In fact, they were no different from present-day jailors or prison guards who are supposed to carry out the sentences imposed on convicts according to the court-rulings.[99] Put simply: It is very likely that the ancient thinkers believed that people suffered malevolent actions of others (including the gods) not only because of some evilness attributable to the abusers but also because of sins attributed to the abused, e.g. for having disturbed the divine order or not observing the duties towards the gods.[100]

The ancient thinkers apparently thought that even the kings were not immune to such maltreatment. They believed that the gods, particularly the head of the pantheon, gave the king the right to rule his subjects because of the king's divine parentage.[101] However, as SELZ 2010, p. 13 has convincingly pointed out, the king needed to prove his legitimacy in order to keep the "Mandate of Heaven" by acting in accordance with the divine order.[102] "Dynastic legitimization is only an additional, not the ultimate source of legitimacy," as Selz observes. If the king had failed to demonstrate his virtue, the gods might give to his subjects the right to revolt against him or allow his foreign enemies to devastate his land. The rebels or the *barbarians* were thus no more than the means for executing the divine punishment of the king. It is also interesting to point out that, in the Mesopotamian world, the righteousness of the individual citizens played no role when it came to the destruction of a city or concerned country. The king alone held full responsibility for the devastation that his monarchy suffered.[103]

---

81 Ištar was furious and [went up] to the heavens,
82 Ištar went [weeping] before her father, Anu.

[98] For Satan, see, e. g., *Anchor Bible Dictionary*, pp. 985–988, "Satan"; *DDD*, pp. 1369–1380, "Satan"; *The Encyclopaedia of Judaism*², pp. 778–783, "Evil and Suffering, Judaic Doctrines of"; *Neues Bibel-Lexikon*, pp. 448–452, "Satan".

[99] For this, cf., KATZ 2003, pp. 127–154, esp. 151–154; and also, GELLER 2007, p. xiii.

[100] It is possible that punishing criminals fell within the authority of the king. For example, in the context of the prosperity amassed as the result of a crime, *Babylonian Theodicy* lines 63–64 warn that the king will burn the rich people (for their undeserved riches).

[101] For gods being the parents of the kings, see, e.g., recently, SALLABERGER 2002, p. 91. Note also, e.g., WILCKE 2002, pp. 64–83; SJÖBERG 1972; STOL 2000, pp. 83–89.

[102] The so-called *Šulgi P*, section b 5–10 gives examples of the obligations of the king towards the gods, (KLEIN 1981, p. 35):

5 Šulgi, the king of a propitious reign,
6 for you (Ninsun) the goddess, may he (Šulgi) *perfectly execute* (lit.: complete) the cultic-norms, which are established for the kingship!
7 may he properly execute the decrees of the gods!
8 may he present you the offerings of the New-Moon and the offerings of the New-Year!
9 may you daily bring his prayers to me!
10 Abundance is my tree which sprouts from the earth like weeds.

[103] For this subject, see ALBREKTSON 1967; SCHAUDIG 2012, pp. 435–440.

The Position of the Author

Von Soden has suggested that, unlike other dialogues, in the *Babylonian Theodicy,* there is no 'winner' of the argument.[104] He further claims that "die Zweifel des Dulders sind auch die des Dichters".[105] Many people must have sensed injustice in the face of the gods, and they might have raised doubts about the meaning of the rituals that they were performing. Thus, so to speak, the sufferer would be the personification of such doubts shared by the many.[106]

However, given the fact that, in the end, the sufferer comes around to fully accepting the friend's position, it seems more likely that the author of the dialogue was actually identifying himself with the friend and not with the sufferer. His faith in the gods and the king forms the backbone of the *Babylonian Theodicy* and this interpretation is reinforced by the acrostic running through the poem, which demonstrates his belief in the gods and the king. The *Babylonian Theodicy* warns the reader against the illusion caused by the wealth and arrogance of the learned, and it also calls for absolute piety to the gods.

The 'Readers' of the *Babylonian Theodicy*

Based on the well-calculated metre with its effectively placed rhymes, one might speculate that this poem was meant to be recited. Yet, the acrostic that consists of 27 signs, each of which is repeated 11 times in one strophe, is clearly a visual device, which must be 'seen' to be appreciated.[107] Given the very low literacy in the ancient Mesopotamian world,[108] we must assume that the 'audience' of this poem was limited to the administrators and bureaucrats,[109] the intellectual and spiritual elites (i.e., priests, scholars[110]) and their apprentices. Judging from the relatively small number of exemplars of the poem that have been unearthed thus far, this *Babylonian Theodicy* was probably not widely known even among the literate communities of Assyria and Babylonia.

As has been established above, the two characters — the sufferer and the friend — are evidently highly educated persons involved in the temple activities. Their title *mūdû*, 'the learned, wise, expert,' which is attested in the main poem as

[104] VON SODEN 1990, p. 145. See also SITZLER 1995, p. 109; BUCCELLATI 1972, p. 171. DENNING-BOLLE 1992, p. 155 suggests that they probably reached a mutual agreement, but she likewise doubts that the friend is indeed won over to the sufferer's position.

[105] VON SODEN, *op cit.* p. 146. See also, BUCCELLATI 1972, p. 172.

[106] BUCCELLATI, *ibid.* p. 171.

[107] DENNING-BOLLE 1987, p. 229; VOGELZANG 1991, p. 51.

[108] For the discussion of literacy in ancient Mesopotamia with references, see, CHARPIN 2010, pp. 53ff, esp., pp. 61–67.

[109] For the terms 'bureaucracy' and 'bureaucrat' instead of 'administration', 'administrative officer' or 'scribe' that are commonly used in Assyriology, see MICHALOWSKI 1987, pp. 45ff.

[110] Many *ummânus* held also the title, *mašmaššu/āšipu*, 'exorcist,' and *kalû*, 'lamentation priest,' i.e., they were also priests.

well as in the *Theodicy Commentary*, speaks in favour of temple scholars or counsellors of the kings (i.e., *ummânu*) as models for the two speakers of the dialogue. One can even speculate that the protagonist was, in fact, an apprentice to the character known as 'the friend'. Thus I believe that the model for the protagonist consisted of trainees in the fields of exorcism, lamentation-priesthood, divination, omen texts,[111] and pharmaceuticals, and that these were 'the targeted readers' of the *Babylonian Theodicy*. Below, I briefly discuss these models of the sufferer and the friend in the *Babylonian Theodicy*. First to be discussed is *ummânu*, the possible model of the friend.

*Ummânu*s

We do not have much information about the scholars from the late second millennium, the time when the *Babylonian Theodicy* was presumably composed.[112] One notable exception, however, is Esagil-kīn-apli, known as the 'author' of the *Sakikkû*-series (the *Diagnostic Handbook*), *Alamdimmû* (the physiognomic omens), and also as the systematiser of the *Beschwörungskunst*. The short summary in the list of incipits of the *Sakikkû*- and *Alandimmû*-series[113] reveals his exact profile.[114] He was a contemporary of Adad-apla-iddina, a king from the Second Dynasty of Isin (1069–1048).[115] He apparently lived in Borsippa and was a 'mainstay' of Sîn, Lisi, and Nanaya.[116] He held different priestly titles[117]: *zabardabbû*, 'bronze bearer,' of Ezida,[118] *pašīšu*-priest of Nabû,[119] *išippu*- and *ramku*-priest[120] of Ninzilzil

[111] For the distinction between *bārûtu* and *ṭupšarrūtu*, see ROCHBERG 2000, p. 361.

[112] See p. xvi above.

[113] FINKEL 1988, pp. 143–159. Finkel bases his edition on two manuscripts: ND 4358+ 4366 and BM 41237+46607+47163. Of these, ND 4358+4366 has been published as CTN 4, no. 71; a copy of the latter manuscript is found in FINKEL, *ibid.*, pp. 156–157. See also, FRAHM 2011, pp. 326–327.

[114] FINKEL, *ibid.*, pp. 148–150.

[115] *Ibid.*, p. 148, A 53–4; B rev 19'.

[116] *Ibid.* A 55–6; B rev 21'. Regarding the translation of *um-mat*, I follow, *CAD* U/W, p. 117, *ummatu* A, b). Note also FINKEL, *ibid.*, p. 149, note 57.

[117] *Ibid.* p. 148, A 55–61; B rev 21'-24'.

[118] The exact meaning of *zabardabbû* is not certain. As a priestly title, note the term *zabardabbi ešarra* applied to Nabû-bēssun and his son, Kiṣir-Aššur, HUNGER 1968, nos. 193–194, 197, 200 and 203. Cf. also, PEDERSÉN 1986, p. 45 and note 22. Nabû-bēssun and Kiṣir-Aššur were also *mašmaš* (*bīt*) *aššuri*, 'the incantation-priest of (the house) of the city Aššur.' For Nabû-bēssun and Kiṣir-Aššur and the text genres found in their "Bibliothek," see MAUL 2010.

[119] Apparently, a *pašīšu* was a kind of priest but its main task was the preparation of offerings. *RlA* 10, p. 630. Priester A. § 5.3.1. Some *pašīšu*-priests received scribal training, RENGER 1969, p. 165. For ^{d}Ì.ZU.ZU = *nabû*, note POMPONIO 1978, pp. 158–159.

[120] The both *išippu* and *ramku* were purification priests. See, *CAD* I/J, p. 242, *išippu* and *CAD* R, p. 126, *ramku*. Note also that the inscription of Esarhaddon recounting his rebuilding of Esagil and Etemenanki refers jointly to *ramku*- and *pašīšu*-priests, LEICHTY 2011, p. 207, vi 19. Note also *Ludlul Bēl Nēmeqi* III — a *ramku*-priest carries out a cleansing ritual for Šubši-mešrê-Šakkan (III 21–28), while a *mašmaššu*-priest from Babylon, who was sent by Marduk himself, performs another ritual act later in the same section (III 40–46). This episode in *Ludlul* also indicates clearly that the *ramku*-priest and the *mašmaššu*-priest acted at different stages, or one might even call it 'on different levels', of the healing process.

(=Nanaya).[121] These titles born by Esagil-kīn-apli suggest that he specialized in exorcism.[122] He was, in fact, credited as the systematiser of the *āšipūtu*, 'the lore of exorcism.'[123] In addition to his priestly titles, he was honoured as the *ummânu* of the lands of Sumer and Akkad.[124] The list of sages (abgal in Sumerian and *ummânu* in Akkadian) from Uruk discussed above[125] also refers to Esagil-kīn-apli as an *ummânu* (line 16).[126]

That Esagil-kīn-apli was simultaneously an incantation-priest and an *ummâmu* is hardly surprising. The *Catalogue of Texts and Authors* referred to above[127] reveals that the 'authors' of the different texts were *ummânu* who were, at one and the same time, mostly either *kalû*-priests or *mašmaššu*-priests, with the exception of the god Ea and the legendary sage Oannes-Adapa.[128] For example, *Catalogue of Texts and Authors* section VI line 10 refers to Sîn-leqi-unninni as the author of the *Gilgameš* series.[129] Sîn-leqi-unninni is listed as ^{lú}MA[Š.MAŠ], i.e. an 'inca[ntation-priest].' Note also line 1 of the same section that refers to Bulluṭsa-rabi, the author of the syncretistic hymn to Gula and Ninurta. He too is referred to as ^{lú}MAŠ.MAŠ ^{lú}U[M.ME.A ...], an 'incantation-priest, *u[mmânu* of GN].'[130]

Most of our knowledge about the scholars comes from seventh century Assyria. Their activities during the reigns of the Neo-Assyrian kings Esarhaddon and Aššurbanipal are particularly well documented in their frequent correspondence with the kings.[131]

For example, in SAA 10, no. 160, a letter sent to the Assyrian king (probably Aššurbanipal),[132] a certain Marduk-šāpik-zēri, apparently a Babylonian, reports an astrological omen and his interpretation on it.[133] He further requests the king to allow him to keep watching the stars of the sky (SAA 10, no. 160, obv 35). His claim to have mastered the omen series *Enūma Anu Enlil* is thus not surprising. However, he further states that he also has studied (obv 42: *altasi*, literally, 'recite, read aloud') additional omen texts — *Šumma Izbu*-series, [*Kataduqqû*-series,

[121] Ninzilzil is Emesal form of Nanaya. See, *RlA* 9, p. 146, Nanaja, § 2.

[122] Judging from the titles, *zabardabbû*, *pašīšu*, *išippu*, and *ramku*, it is evident that he specialized in cleansing rituals which normally belonged to the lore of *mašmaššu*/*āšipu*.

[123] GELLER 2000, p. 248, line 27.

[124] FINKEL 1998, p. 148, A 60–61//B 24'.

[125] VAN DIJK 1962, pp. 44ff.

[126] The name of the king whom Esagil-kīn-apli served as the royal counsellor is not preserved in this list.

[127] For the edition, see LAMBERT 1962.

[128] LAMBERT, *ibid.*, p. 64, 1) line 4 and 6.

[129] *Ibid.*, p. 66.

[130] For the edition, see LAMBERT 1967. A scholar specialized in professions other than *mašmaššūtu* and *kalûtu* could also be an *ummânu*. For example, Gimil-Nanaya is listed as ^{lú}ḪAL ^{lú}UM.ME.A TIN.TIR^{ki}, 'haruspex, *ummânu* of Babylon,' *ibid.*, VII) 7.

[131] For the editions of these letters, see SAA 10.

[132] HUNGER 1987, p. 162 dates this letter to the reign of Šamaš-šuma-ukīn (i.e., Aššurbanipal was the king of Assyria). Brinkman believes that he was active during the reign of Esarhaddon, *PNA*, p. 726. GELLER 2010, p. 187 note 101, suggests that this Marduk-šāpik-zēri is the same person known from the Egibi archive. According to JURSA 2005, pp. 100–101, he was active since the time of Šamaš-šuma-ukīn and had a temple-enterer's prebend.

[133] SAA 10, no. 160, obv 11–29. For the omen, see GELLER 2010, pp. 75–77.

Alan]*dimmû*-series and *Nigdimdimmû*-series (obv 40–42). Very interestingly, he also claims that he has mastered his father's profession, *kalûtu*, 'the art of lamentation,' (obv 36–37), and that he is competent in diverse cleansing rituals (like *mīs pî*, 'mouth-washing'; *takpirti ekurri*, 'purification rite of temples,' obv 38–39). Given the fact that he recommends 20 *ummânu*s from different disciplines who have studied with him (obv 47 and rev 35), it is evident that Marduk-šāpik-zēri himself must have been an *ummânu*, 'scholar.'

The multi-talents of Assyrian royal scholars suggest that they were required to master not only one discipline but also to gain a wide range of knowledge in order to offer the king advice in diverse fields,[134] above all, those concerning religious and health issues. For example, Esarhaddon's chief exorcist, Adad-šumu-uṣur gave advice on health issues concerning the king himself as well as his family members;[135] his advice also concerned a drug (literally 'plant'[136]) to be administered to the crown prince (SAA 10, no. 191). Often he recited rituals (SAA 10, no. 200) or 'prescribed' incantations to be used during the *Namburbi*-rituals (SAA 10, nos. 194 and 201[137]). Adad-šumu-uṣur also supervised the substitute-king rituals (SAA 10, nos. 189, 219–221). In addition to giving health advice and supervising the rituals, he also sent astrological reports (SAA 10, nos. 197–198, 206, 216, 224–228). Thus, Adad-šumu-uṣur's letters well demonstrate the wide range of his knowledge similar to that of Esagil-kīn-apli and Marduk-šāpik-zēri.

Despite the fact that these *ummânu*s worked very close to the sovereigns, there is no sign that they abused their rich knowledge of the various scholarly disciplines for their own interests, e.g. to seize power and wealth.[138] The scholars in the service of the king remained very loyal servants.[139] Even when they had to offer advice to the king on the state matters[140] or the king's personal issues,[141] they

---

[134] See, for example, the recent study of the scholars from the descendants of Gabbu-ilāni-ēreš, the chief *ummânu* of Tukulti-Ninurta II (890–884) and Aššurnaṣirpal II (883–859 BCE), ŠAŠJOVÁ 2010. Note also, PEŠÍKOVÁ 1985; LUUKKO 2007. Cf. also, FRAHM 2011, p. 19.

[135] See, e.g., GELLER 2010, pp. 86–88; ŠAŠJOVÁ 2010, 122–126.

[136] For use of plants as *materia medica*, i.e., medicines, see GELLER 2010, pp. 19–21; 62–65 and *passim*.

[137] See, PARPOLA 1983, p. 148, notes on no. 160 rev 4'.

[138] *Ibid.*, p. XVIII.

[139] *Ibid.*, p. XX.

[140] Note, for instance, the comments of Adad-šumu-uṣur on Esarhaddon's nomination of Aššurbanipal as the crown prince and Šamaš-šuma-ukīn as the king of Babylon. see , SAA 10, no. 185, 5b–6:

> *šá ina* AN-*e la e-piš-u-ni* LUGAL *be-lí ina qaq-qí-ri e-tap-áš*
> What has not been done in the heavens, the king, my lord, has done on earth.

This was probably meant to be a criticism of the king's decision. Nonetheless, Adad-šumu-uṣur praises Esarhaddon's act in the rest of the letter. The *ummânus* are also listed along with the royal family and provincial governors as potential kingmakers, SAA 2, no. 6, 79.

[141] Adad-šumu-uṣur, chief exorcist of Esarhaddon, referred to above, sent a letter to the king giving advice on how to overcome his depression, SAA 10, no. 196. In this letter, he says to the king, rev. 14ff:

> *mi*[*l-ku dam-q*]*u iḫ-ḫa-sa-sa ka-*[*ru-u i*]*k-ki la a-*[*ka*]*-lu la šá-tu-u ṭè-e-mu ú-šá-šá mur-ṣu ú-rad an-ni-tu* LUGAL *a-na* ⸢ÌR⸣-[*šu*] ⸢*liš*⸣-[*m*]*i*

maintained their humble attitude to the sovereign and observed "the overwhelmingly passive and "academic" nature of their advisory role."[142] The king always had the last word. Their duty, therefore, was to protect the king and his interests with their scholarly knowledge gained by studying the "Scriptures" which had been compiled by the god Enki/Ea, the legendary sage Adapa, and the scholars of earlier generations.[143] As Parpola says, the "Scriptures" were the "ultimate source of wisdom, the validity of which was never questioned."[144]

Apprentices

We now turn our attention to the trainees of the *ummânus* who were probably the models of the sufferer of the *Babylonian Theodicy*. Particularly interesting, is the manner in which the "Scriptures" were taught and learned. How did the trainees acquire their knowledge of the different disciplines of exorcism, lamentation-priesthood, divination, omen texts, and medical lore? In addition to basic training in reading and writing, e.g., signs, vocabulary, and the different formulae of the documents, what did the trainees in the schools in Babylonia learn?

Speaking of the 'schools' during the early second millennium, MICHALOWSKI 1987, p. 52 describes their function as follows:

> The school was an ideological moulder of minds, the place where future members of the bureaucracy were socialized, where they received a common stock of ideas and attitudes which bound them together as a class and in many ways separated them from their original backgrounds.

I agree with this definition of the school as the "ideological moulder of minds", and I believe that it can also be applied to the schools of the first millennium BCE. For example, judging from the contents of the preserved school tablets, the students at the scribe school in Babylon acquired not only the basic skills of writing but also absorbed the prevailing ideology and doctrine, which centred on Marduk,

---

> G[ood ad]vice is to be heard: restlessness, not eating and not drinking disturbs the *mind* and illness will come down. In this matter, the king should listen to [his se]rvant.

Note also Adad-šumu-uṣur's advice for Esarhaddon's critically ill child in *ibid*., no. 187.

[142] PARPOLA 1983, p. XVIII. See also, PEČÍRKOVÁ 1985, pp. 167–168.

[143] Note the *Catalogue of Texts and Authors*, LAMBERT 1962. According to this list, *āšpūtu*, *kalûtu*, *Enūma Anu Enlil*, *Alamdimmû*, *Sagitinutila*, *Sakikkû*, *Kataduggû*, *Lugale*, *Angimdimma* are credited to Ea, *ibid*., p. 64, segment 1) 1–4.

[144] PARPOLA 1983, p. XXI.

VAN DER TOORN 2007, p. 27 asserts that "[t]he secret nature of their knowledge was a matter of importance primarily to the scribes themselves. It gave them a sense of superiority with little effect outside their own circles." Given the primal purpose of the scholars/counsellors to support the king, it is self-evident that their scholarly knowledge had little *DIRECT* effect on the rest of the society. On the other hand, the ancient thinkers must have believed that the king's correct conduct with respect to the divine order might affect the state of the land — if the king failed to keep the divine law, the nation might face the threat of divine punishment, e.g., war, epidemic, natural disasters, and so forth. It was also in the national interest to keep the well-being of the king, so to speak. Although van der Toorn's view on the secret knowledge is correct in reality, the ancient scholars must have believed that they possessed pre-eminent knowledge that might affect the stability of a nation.

the supreme god of Babylonia in the first millennium.[145] During what P. Gesche calls the "zweite Stufe",[146] the students then copied excerpts of different 'literary' texts. The most important text studied by the ancient students in Babylon was probably *Enūma Eliš*, the Babylonian Creation Epic. This myth recounts how Marduk became the supreme god and created the world. It also recounts the selection of Babylon as Marduk's earthly residence and as the political centre of the king, Marduk's human deputy. Through *Enūma Eliš*, they learned about the order of the world. Moreover, through copying *Ludlul Bēl Nēmeqi*, the students became familiar with the severity of Marduk's punishment for neglecting the cultic duties but also his power of salvation. They also studied Marduk's divinity by copying canonical prayers and incantations, such as the *Prayers to Marduk nos. 1* and *2*,[147] and the *Utukkū-Lemnūtu* incantations that include the *Marduk's Address to the Demons*.[148]

It is very likely, however, that, at this stage, the students still had only a very limited access to the "Scriptures" as a whole. This is indicated by a survey of the texts used by the *mašmaššu-/āšipu*-priests in antiquity. On the text known to modern scholars as the "*Leitfaden der Beschwörungskunst*" or the *Manual of the Exorcist*, M. J. Geller has identified 98 entries as constituting the obligatory corpora for the *mašmaššu-/āšipu*-priests.[149] Interestingly, P. Gesche has observed[150] that, with the exception of *Maqlû*, *Šurpu*, *Saggigu*-incantations, and *Zipa*-incantations, the remaining texts known from the *Manual* are not attested on the school tablets containing excerpts of different texts, which have been found in Babylon. The same is true for other disciplines. No known school exercise preserves, for example, *Enūma Anu Enlil*, liver-omens or medical texts. This fact supports the conjecture that at this second stage of their scribal education, the students were still not qualified enough to have full access to the main Scriptures of the different professions.

---

[145] Cf., GESCHE 2001, p. 211. For the text corpora that the students used for learning, see *ibid.*, pp. 173–178. Note also, VAN DER TOORN 1991, p. 72 where he states that "the future scribes ... received a general education in humanities."

[146] GESCHE 2001, pp. 172ff. For a similar two stage learning system in the Old-Babylonian period, see, e.g., VELDHUIS 2004, pp. 39–47; 60–80.

[147] For the *Prayers to Marduk nos. 1* and *2*, see OSHIMA 2011, pp. 137–190; 216–270.

[148] For prayers serving as 'Scriptures,' cf., OSHIMA *ibid.*, pp. 31–32. Cf. also the scribal education system in the early second millennium outlined in VOLK 2011, pp. 293–299.

[149] For the edition, see JEAN 2006, pp. 63–82; GELLER 2000, pp. 242–254. Note also the list of the texts on GELLER, *ibid.*, pp. 256–258. In addition to Geller's copies, note also the new duplicate from Uruk, VON WEIHER 1998, no. 231. Geller and Jean refer to an additional manuscript from Assur A 366 in Istanbul, but they do not use it for their editions.

As it is clear from the rubric — "incipits of the series on the art of exorcism drawn up for instruction and *testing*, all to be read aloud", the *mašmaššu-/āšipu*-priests were required to master all of these texts contained in this ancient 'syllabus' for the exorcism. GELLER 2010, p. 123; JEAN 2006, p. 62. For the interpretation of *tāmartu* ($IGI.DU_8$), as 'test' instead of more common usages of the word with the meanings 'reference, seeing, reading,' see GELLER, *ibid.*, p. 137. Incidentally, while JEAN *ibid.*, p. 72 and FRAHM 2011, p. 325 take this rubric as referring to the text above it, others like FINKEL 1988, p. 150 and BEAULIEU 2000, p. 15 suggest that it is the heading for the text following it.

[150] GESCHE 2001, p. 172. Likewise, she has identified no omen texts such as *Šumma Ālu* and *Šumma Izbu* within her text corpus. See the catalogue of the texts and the index on *ibid.*, pp. 669–792; 806–820.

Thus, it seems that, in addition to the second stage of scribal education, there must have been a third stage before a trainee became fully qualified as a specialist.[151] Gesche has already pointed out in her study of school texts from first millennium Babylonia that the archaeologists have unearthed a number of tablets copied by *ṭupšarru ṣeḫru*, 'junior scribe,' and *šamallû*, 'novice,' that contain not mere excerpts but full texts of different genres.[152] It seems, therefore, that, during this third stage of their "*Fachausbildung*", the selected apprentices received direct instructions from 'professors' (*ummânu*) who specialized in the different disciplines.[153]

SAA 10, no. 160, discussed above, best illustrates the training system during this phase of *Fachausbildung*.[154] In this letter recommending his apprentices for the king's service, the *ummânu* Marduk-šāpik-zēri, states, in lines 47ff., that they had studied with him (*ittija liginnu* [...] *ilsû*)[155]. Concerning his first candidate, for example, he remarks, (rev 1–3):

1 [..., who f]rom Elam has crossed over, the lore of extispicy
2 [has *fully mastered*], and [*Enūma A*]*nu Enlil*, ancient and Sumerian commentaries,
3 [the secret of the heavens and the ea]rth, *knows* he *very well*. He would be *useful* for the king, my lord.

Marduk-šāpik-zēri also recommends an additional 19 specialists in similar manner, so, for instance, concerning the last three persons in the list (rev. 30–34):

30 Lā-baši *knows very well* the series of exorcism. He would be *useful* for the king, my lord.
31 Kudurru *knows very well* extispicy; the series *Enūma Anu Enlil*
32 has he read. He would be *useful* for the king, my lord.
33 Aḫa-Šubši, physician, he is very capable.
34 He would be *useful* for <the king>, my lord.

---

[151] *Ibid.*, pp. 210–218.

[152] Note also the medical texts published in FINKEL 2000. Unlike more common formulae of Mesopotamian medical texts, only a few recipes or treatments for different illnesses are recorded on each tablet. Based on this, Finkel has concluded that these texts were exercises of the trainees for the *asûtu*, 'medicine,' and *ašipūtu*, 'exorcism,' *ibid.*, pp. 137–147, esp. 138–139. Note also, JURSA 1999, pp. pp. 12–31, esp. 12 and 26–31.

[153] GESCHE *op. cit.*, pp. 213–216. Note also FINKEL *op. cit.*, p. 141.

[154] See pp. xxxviii–xxxix above.

[155] The expression, *liginnu šasû/qabû* literally means 'to read aloud a (*type*) of tablets.' The word *liginnu* in the later period referred to "tablets containing excerpts of literary works for recitation and teaching," BEAULIEU, 1992, p. 103 and note 16. For *liginnu šasû/qabû* being an idiom for 'to study, learn,' see PARPOLA 1983, p. 39, rev 9 (commentary on letter LAS 34 (+) 49); BEAULIEU, *ibid.*, pp. 103–105. Note also the incipit of the "*Leitfaden der Beschwörungskunst*" (KAR 44) cited above, where 'to read aloud' is also used in the sense of 'to learn.'

However, *liginnu šasû/qabû*, does not always refer to education in secret lore. Note, for example, SAA 16, no. 28, the letter sent by Šerū'a-ēṭirat, the eldest daughter of Esarhaddon to Libbali-šarrat, Aššurbanipal's wife. In this letter, Šerū'a-ēṭirat asks Libbali-šarrat: *a-ta-a ṭup-pi-ki la ta-šaṭ-ṭi-ri* IM.GID (=*liginna*)-*ki la ta-qab-bi-i*, 'Why don't you write the tablet (by yourself) and recite (i.e., learn) your exercise?' For this interpretation, I follow, LIVINGSTONE 2007, pp. 104–105. Given the context, it is evident that the Assyrian princess is not questioning the queen's knowledge of divine secrets but simply encouraging her to learn the scribal art. LIVINGSTONE, *ibid.*, p. 105.

This letter clearly suggests that, with the words *ittija liginnu … ilsû*, literally 'they recited *liginnu*-tablets with me,' Marduk-šāpik-zēri is actually referring to the teaching method. It is very likely that, after the "zweite Schulstufe," only a chosen group of students received further education directly from the *ummânu* 'professor' in order to specialize in one of the fields of divination, omen texts, exorcism, medicine and lamentation-priesthood.[156]

Given the excessive use of Sumerian words/Sumerograms in addition to rare signs/phonetic values in the omens texts (*Šumma Ālu*, *Šumma Izbu*, *Enūma Anu Enlil*, *Alamdimmû*), the *Diagnostic-Handbook* (*Sakikkû*-series) and ritual instructions, one may surmise that the *ummânus* taught the apprentices the correct readings/interpretation of these texts by using ancient commentaries.[157] A hint to such method of education is found in a letter sent to Aššurbanipal by his tutor Balasî, SAA 10, no. 60, obv 10–rev 14:

> … there is a particular tablet [in] which the […]s are written, and I am now sending it to the king. The king should have a look. Maybe the scribe who reads to the king did not understand.
>
> *Šumma Izbu* is difficult to interpret. The first time that I come before the king, my lord, I shall (personally) show how, — with [i.e. using] this tablet that I am sending to the king, my lord, — the omen is written.
>
> Really, [someone] who has [not] had (the meaning) pointed out to him cannot possibly understand it.

This letter suggests that the student (in this particular case, Aššurbanipal) had read *Šumma Izbu* probably with the aid of a commentary while his teacher (in this particular case, Balasî) was explaining how to interpret the texts.[158]

The Person Qualified for the "Scriptures"

In order to avoid misuse of the sacred knowledge, the "Scriptures" had to be kept away from the eyes of the wider public.[159] As it has already been claimed by modern scholars, the colophons labelling these texts as *niṣirtu* or *pirištu*, 'secret, ta-

---

[156] SAA 16, no. 65 reports that Parruṭu, a goldsmith of the household of the queen, bought a Babylonian, apparently as a slave, and made him teach his son the exercise tablet containing exorcism (*āšipūtu*), and also reveal omens from divination and a section of astrology, (lines 2–11). Clearly the unnamed sender of this letter took the action of Parruṭu to be an irregular behaviour for a goldsmith or even a breach of the scholarly principle and, therefore, a threat to the king. The uses of *uk-tal-li-mu-šu*, 'he has shown to him,' and *lu e-ta-mar*, 'he has indeed seen,' are reminiscent of the *Geheimwissen* colophon, probably hinting at the restricted access to the scholarly lore imposed by it. See, LENZI 2008, pp. 155–156.

[157] See, e.g., MEIER 1937–39, pp. 239–240; WEIDNER 1959–60, pp. 151–152; HUNGER 1976, p. 13; GESCHE 2001, p. 213. Cf. also FRAHM 2011, pp. 329–330, 336–338. Note also the list of the tablets bearing colophons of Anu-ikṣur, an incantation-priest from Uruk, on HUNGER, *ibid.*, p. 12. As Hunger points out, many commentaries copied by him were labelled as *malsūtu*, "Vorlesung," (=lecture) *ibid.* Note especially that, among these commentaries for *malsūtu*, nos. 33, 49 and 50 were copied by Anu-ikṣur when he was still a *mašmaššu ṣeḫru*, 'junior incantation-priest.' Note also VON WEIHER 1988, no. 99, which contains a commentary on *Šumma Ālu*, which Anu-ikṣur copied during his apprenticeship for his "(Vor)lesung."

[158] FRAHM 2011, p. 203.

[159] See, most recently, LENZI 2008, pp. 160ff.

boo,' or better known by the German terminology, *Geheimwissen*, were meant to limit access to these Scriptures and, therefore, to the knowledge they contain.[160] The rather excessive use of rare Sumerograms in the omen texts and ritual instructions must also have contributed to make understanding of these texts difficult.[161] PONGRATZ-LEISTEN 1999, p. 291 explains that, during the reigns of Esarhaddon and Aššurbanipal, the encoding, i.e., these colophons and the use of Sumerian/Sumerogram and rare phonetic values, "nicht nur aus dem Bedürfnis nach sozialem Prestigegewinn und sozialer Abgrenzung geschah,[162] sondern im direkten Verbund mit den Mechanismen des Machterwerbs und Macherhalts von seiten des Königtums zu sehen ist." Therefore, she further asserts that only the scholars had access to "Wissen und die gesamte Deutungskultur" because they could be controlled by the king through the "Institution des Loyalitätseides."[163]

It appears however, that the scholars also, on their own initiative, promoted the secrecy of their knowledge. These colophons of *Geheimwissen* normally begin with the fixed instruction, *mūdû mūdâ likallim lā mūdû lā immar/ai īmur*,[164] i.e. 'may the learned[165] show (this only) to the learned; the unlearned shall not/should not see (it).' This standardised phrase is followed by *niṣirtu* or *pirištu* 'secret, restriction,' with a further definition.[166] This phraseology, *mūdû mūdâ likallim lā*

[160] As it has already been noted by Borger, there is a problem of multifaceted inconsistency of the texts that the *Geheimwissen* colophons are attached to, *RlA* 3, p. 190, Geheimwissen: "Gewiß haben die Babylonier and Assyrer noch zahlreiche weitere Texte als G[heimwissen] betrachtet, die uns durch das Fehlen der Kolophone nicht mehr als solche kenntlich sind. Warum bestimmte Texte als G. betrachtet wurden, andere ganz ähnliche, manchemal sogar zu der gleichen Tafelserie gehörige, jedoch nicht, entzieht sich nicht selten unserem Verständnis. Mehrfach erscheint uns auch das so sorgfältig gehütete G. ziemlich uninteressant oder gar wertlos." See also, PONGRATZ-LEISTEN 1999, p. 290; LENZI 2008, pp. 204; 206.

[161] For the use of difficult signs and rare sound values as means of demarcation from the daily writing usage, cf., VELDHUIS 1997, pp. 145–146; BÖCK 2000, p. 43; LENZI 2008, p. 148.

[162] On this point, see BURKERT 1995, p. 96: "Mysterienweihe also bedeutet die Gewinnung und Sicherung eines Privilegs, garantiert durch ein 'Wissen' um das Paßwort der Gruppe, der man zugehört ... So 'weiß' der eleusinische Myste, daß er 'Geschlechtsgenosse der Götter' ist, zur 'Verwandtschaft' gehört."

[163] PONGRATZ-LEISTEN 1999, p. 318,

[164] See *RlA* 3, p. 189, Geheimwissen; *RlA* 12, p. 270, Schreiber C, § 1.3; LENZI 2008, pp. 168–174; 216–219.

[165] Borger, translates *mūdû*, "Eingeweiht," *RlA* 3, p. 189. On the other hand, LENZI 2008, p. 206 translates, "*qualified* scholar" and further claims that the term *mūdû* refers to the scholars who "had mastered the material [of different disciplines] and knew how to use it appropriately," *Ibid.*, p. 207. However, as already discussed above, a significantly large number of copies of the texts belonging to the "Scriptures" were actually made by the apprentices, thus suggesting that the persons who copied these tablets were still in their "*Ausbildung*". In other words, although *mūdû* in the *Geheimwissen* colophon were most likely the persons qualified to get further training after they had mastered writing skills and doctrines, they were not yet "*qualified* scholars" as such, like Lenzi believes. For further discussion, see below.

[166] These secrets are further defined by the terminology specifying the genres. These terminologies can be divided into three different categories:

A): divine name(s). The names of gods are: Anu and Enlil; Enza, Maḫza, and Kizaza; the Great Enlil, Marduk; Anu, Enlil, and Ea, the great gods; Enlil, Igigi-gods, and Anunnaki-gods; Šullat and Ḫaniš; Šamaš and Adad, *RlA* 3 Geheimwissen, p. 189. Note also, LENZI 2008, pp. 171–174.

B): field of specialization (i.e., *bārûtu*, 'divination;' *āšipūtu*, 'exorcism;' *ummânūtu*, 'scholar's lore').

mūdû lā immar/ai īmur, suggests two things: 1) 'the learned' refers to a status recognized by other persons sharing the same status as scholars; 2) 'the learned' held the ultimate responsibility for presenting the tablets belonging to the special categories, i.e., for revealing the secret lore.

A warning against allowing an unqualified person to gain access to the secret lore is also found in the list of the *Sakikkû*-series and the *Alandimmû*-series.[167] After the statement about Esagil-kīn-apli's editorial work, it states as follows, B 27'–28':[168]

B 27' Do not neglect your knowledge. He who does not *attain*(?)[169] knowledge should not read aloud (i.e., learn) the *Sakikkû*,
B 28' nor should he recite (i.e., learn) the *Alandimmû*. ...

Just like the *Geheimwissen* colophon, this instruction in the list of the *Sakikkû*-and *Alandimmû*-series prohibits access by those who do not possess the "knowledge".

Although, as Pongratz-Leisten has asserted, the oath of loyalty to the king taken by the ancient scholars probably prohibited them from spreading the secret knowledge of divination, exorcism, and so forth,[170] I believe that the recognition of a person's status as *mūdû*, 'the learned,' by fellow *mūdû* played a more important role in the transmission of the scholarly knowledge.[171] Given the fact, established above, that the majority of the Scriptures were not revealed to the second stage students in the scribal school, it is evident that writing skill as such was not the key qualification for access to the secret lore. What then was the qualification for being recognized as a *mūdû* and gaining access to the ancient wisdom?

To master and conserve such wisdom, the scholars and their apprentices must have been required to demonstrate their absolute loyalty and trust in the gods, and this for two reasons; 1) the knowledge of these five fields is attributed to the god Enki/Ea and the legendary sage Adapa; and 2) the knowledge itself is closely related to the divine world and the rituals.[172] Probably reverence towards the gods also prevented misuse of such knowledge. But how did this knowledge foster such a strong devotion to the gods?

I believe that the answer is found in the *Babylonian Theodicy*; indeed, one may even claim that the *Babylonian Theodicy* itself is the answer. As noted above, the friend repeatedly emphasises the importance of the rituals while he also states that man is not capable of understanding the divine order, plan and will. The ancient thinkers must have perceived the different rituals — recitation of prayers, lamen-

C): other attributions (i.e., *šarrūtu*, 'kingship,' *šamû u erṣetu*, 'the heavens and the earth;' and *apkallu*, 'sage'). See, *RlA* 3, pp. 189–190.

For a recent detailed treatment of this categorization, see, LENZI 2008, pp. 168ff.; 216–219.

[167] FINKEL 1988, pp. 148–150.

[168] = FINKEL *ibid.*, pp. 148–149.

[169] As for the interpretation of GUB.BI, I follow, FINKEL, *ibid.*, 148, note 51.

[170] PONGRATZ-LEISTEN 1999, p. 318.

[171] Cf., the observation on the *sythema* and *symbolon* in the secrecy in the Classic literature by BURKERT 1995, p. 97: "Es ging nicht um den Inhalt eines 'Wissens', sondern um die Einzigartigkeit des Zugangs, die zu verteidigen war." This observation might be applicable to the interpretation of the secret knowledge in ancient Mesopotamia.

[172] For this, see p. xxxviii above.

tations, and praises to the gods as well as offerings and sacrifices — not only as the means for maintaining the gods' satisfaction with humankind but also as the vehicle for reaching the state of pure devotion and piety towards the divine. Although such devoutness might not always lead the ancients to the material riches promised by the ancient teachings and proverbs, it could very well bring them to the wealth of divine wisdom, the everlasting principle.[173] On the other hand, the material riches that the sufferer desires could very well corrupt a man's mind, elicit a malicious appetite, and eventually lead him away from the gods. Thus the friend tells the protagonist in lines 219–220 of the *Babylonian Theodicy*:

> Follow the tradition of the god, keep his cultic rites.
> [*Leave* …] and the evildoers; be ready for well-being.

This idea is not unique to the *Babylonian Theodicy*. The importance of piety and divine blessing as its reward, as well as the teaching as the base of the reverence are also taught in the *Counsels of Wisdom*, lines 135–147:[174]

> Everyday, worship your god
> (with) offering (and) benediction, (they are) worthy of (lit.: proper to) incense offering.
> You should *present* (lit.: have) free-will offering to your god.
> This is proper to godhead.
> When, petitioning, beseeching, and *showing respect*,
> (and) barley, you offer to him (the personal god), he will reward you in full,
> and moreover, you will *be guided correctly by* the god (lit.: you will march with the god).
> In your learning, look into the tablet:
> Reverence begets *blessing*;
> offering prolongs vigour;
> and a supplication absolves sins.
> The one who reveres the gods will not be deprived of *blessing*;
> the life of the one who reveres Anunnaki-gods will be long.

Thus I propose that the primary intention of the *Babylonian Theodicy* was to teach the apprentices of scholars the value of absolute piety to the gods and importance of the rituals even in the face of evils. The sufferer's rejection by the friend is, moreover, a warning to those who refuse to accept the principle of the divine ordinance. There was no place for godless fools in the scholarly world of the ancients.[175]

---

[173] Cf., the observation by van der Toorn on the wisdom taught in the Standard Babylonian version of the *Gilgamesh Epic*: "He [i.e., Gilgamesh] proposes a superior wisdom by holding out secret knowledge from before the flood as the only antidote to death. Such knowledge does not prevent anyone from dying, but its comfort is more satisfying than hedonism," VAN DER TOORN 2007, p. 25.

[174] The last edition, LAMBERT 1960, pp. 104–105. A similar notion is also found in another text giving a counsel, the *Counsels of a Pessimist*, lines 9–13, see *ibid*., pp. 108–109.

[175] A warning against the incompetence of an *ummânu* is known from a text fragment found in Uruk, HUNGER 1974, no. 2 (W. 22289). This is probably a historical epic on the reign of Šulgi (2094–2047 BCE). In this text, Lu-Nanna, the counsellor (*ummânu*) of Šulgi, is blamed for altering the cult order of Anu and the scholars' secret knowledge (lines 11–14). It even states that he was not worthy of the secret knowledge (line 14: [*ni*]-*ṣir-ti* ^{lú}*um-man-nu šá la si-mat*, 'the secret (lore) of the scholars that was not suitable (for him)'). Lu-Nanna apparently was blamed for writing Šulgi's in-

Concluding Remarks

The *Babylonian Theodicy* explores the timeless questions about unrewarded piety in a very abstract manner. Although different didactic texts promise of wealth as the result of one's piety, many people must have seen that the powerful and rich often amassed their fortunes without showing reverence to the gods, often, indeed, by the felonious methods, as the sufferer argues in the *Babylonian Theodicy*. It is almost certain that injustice before the gods was very frequently questioned in antiquity not only by the learned elites but also by people belonging to other social classes. The *Babylonian Theodicy* offers a degree of consolation for unrewarded piety. Through the mouth of the friend, the author argues that possessions not gained by means of piety are not everlasting and that godless rogues will be punished for their crimes. On the other hand, the author insists that piety will be rewarded with everlasting blessing (e.g., line 66). If my interpretation of the text is correct, the author understands everlasting blessing to mean not material riches but rather divine wisdom.

Because of its lack of concreteness, it is very hard to grasp the message in the *Babylonian Theodicy*. The name of the god whom the speakers worshipped might have given a slightly better feeling of tangibleness to the *Babylonian Theodicy* but the author seems to have deliberately avoided references to any particular deity. At least in the preserved portions of the text, aside from rare references to the mother-goddess Mami (or Aruru), the divine king Enlil (under his byname Narru)

---

scriptions and tablets (i.e., instructions) for the cleansing rituals of the gods making use of lies and villainy (lines 16–17). For the interpretation, I follow CAVIGNEAUX 2005, p. 65. Incidentally WILCKE 1982, p. 144, offers a different restoration for the beginning of line 17: [NU].LUḪ.ḪA ([*nu*]*ḫurat*), 'Stinkkraut,' Wilcke's suggestion, however does not yield a good sense. As a result, a god, (probably Anu) imposed on Šulgi a severe punishment (18–19). It is very likely, although not conclusive due to the lacunae, that the purpose of this text was to explain the death of Šulgi, possibly violent one. If my interpretation of this text fragment is correct, the ancient thinkers from Uruk evidently blamed Lu-Nanna for Šulgi's adversity instead of the king himself. I thank K. Lämmerhirt for drawing my attention to this HUNGER 1974, no. 2. For the death of Šulgi, see MICHALOWSKI 1977; HOROWITZ and WATSON 1991, pp. 413–416, esp. p. 415 note 17. The *Esagil-Chronicle* also recounts that Šulgi altered the cleansing ritual of Esagil and evoked Marduk's anger. For this, see SCHAUDIG 2012, pp. 433–441. It is now commonly accepted that the ascent of Šulgi to the heavens is a euhemerism, see, e.g., WILCKE 1988, esp. pp. 250ff; SELZ 2000, pp. 967–976; *Idem* 2008, p. 21. On the scholars as being the real authors of the Mesopotamian royal inscriptions, see CHARPIN 2010, pp. 299 and 236–237 with further references.

One may speculate that this text, HUNGER 1974, no. 2, was used to teach the apprentices what might happen when they got their hands on the scholars' secret knowledge without proper teaching. It is noteworthy that this manuscript (W. 22289) was copied by Anu-balassu-iqbi as part of his education (rev 7'–8'). Incidentally, the tablet itself was a property of Anu-aḫa-ušabši, his father, *mašmaššu*, and *šešgallu* of the Rēš temple of Uruk.

It seems that, in the first millennium scribal tradition, Lu-Nanna, who is best known as the author of the series *Etana* (LAMBERT 1962, p. 66, VI 11), is presented as an unsuccessful scholar. For example, VON WEIHER 1983, no. 8 (the *Bīt Mēseri*) refers to the antediluvian 4 abgal/*apkallu*s (Nungal-piriggal, Piriggal-nungal, Piriggal-abzu, and Lu-Nanna) during the time when they were abgal/*apkallu*, the world order was disturbed (col. i 14–27). As the last of the four abgal/*apkallus*, Lu-Nanna is referred to in col. i 24–27. He is said to be only 2/3 abgal/*apkallu*. It also recounts that he let the Ušumgallu-dragon come out of the temple of Ištar of Šulgi, apparently an allusion to a disaster. On the other hand, the seven abgal/*apkallu*s before the deluge were pure *purādu*-fish lived in the sea and kept the world in order (col. i 1–13). For the text, see also, REINER 1961; BORGER 1974, p. 187. Note also CAVIGNEAUX 2005, pp. 68–69.

and Ea, the god of wisdom and life, (under his very rare byname Zulummaru) — all in the context of mankind in general and its creation, no particular divine names are mentioned. And it is striking that in the case of Enlil and Ea, the author does not refer to them by their principal names, Enlil/Ellil and Ea, or by their most common Sumerograms ^{d}IDIM and ^{d}BAD, or even by their better attested bynames, Nunnamnir (Enlil) and Nudimmud (Ea). In fact, the bynames Narru nor Zulummaru are not attested at all in the preserved portions of the *Canonical God-list* that goes under the title An=*Anum*. The same is true for the Mother-Goddess. Although Aruru and Mami are commonly attested in the Sumerian and the early Babylonian literature, Aruru appears as the 25th name of Bēlet-ilī and Mami is listed as her very last name (the 45th name) in An=*Anum*.[176] It seems, therefore, that the author deliberately tried to mask the identities of the great gods of the Mesopotamian pantheon.

Probably more significant is the author's use of the common nouns *ilu* and *ištar*/*iltu* without relating them to any particular deities. Theoretically, one might surmise that the *Babylonian Theodicy* is dealing with private religion and that these words (*ilu* and *ištar*/*iltu*) refer to the personal gods. However, this conjecture is open to criticism because, in the preserved portions of the text, there is no attestation of the personalized terms *ilī* or *ištarī*/*iltī* (literally, my god and my goddess), which normally indicate the personal-gods. Of course, it would still be possible to interpret the common terms *ilu* and *ištar*/*iltu* as meaning '*THE* god' and '*THE* goddess' since the Akkadian language has no articles. However, in the preserved portions of the text, there are no clues as to which deities the author might have intended under these common terms *ilu* and *ištar*/*iltu*. In principle, these terms could refer to any individual god or goddess in the Mesopotamian pantheon, or they could refer to all the gods and goddesses collectively.[177] From the latter usage, it would be a small relatively step to developing an abstract notion of "divinity" or "deity" as such, no longer individuated after the manner of classical polytheism. If that be the case, the *Babylonian Theodicy* could well represent a significant advance in the direction of developing a monotheistic theology, as I hope to show in a future publication.

The author left his 'signature' in the form of acrostic as discussed above. We know that (E)saggil-kīna-ubbib was an incantation-priest (*mašmaššu*). The acrostic also displays his piety to the gods and his trust in the king. In addition, judging from the author lists from Kouyunjik and the list of the scholars from Uruk, he was most likely a scholar who lived in the eleventh century BCE. Yet, other than that, in the surviving portions of the text as such, there is no clue to its historical background. There are neither personal nor geographical names in the text. We have no idea which god the author worshipped. By carefully removing the identities of the gods and the characters of the poem, the author created enduring kind of universal dogma applicable to any of the cults and anyone living in Mesopotamia.[178]

---

[176] LITKE 1998, pp. 69, 72.

[177] BOTTÉRO 1977, p. 38.

[178] MATTINGLY 1990, p. 326 believes that "the purpose of such works [including the *Babylonian Theodicy*] was to affirm the trustworthiness of the traditional dogmas."

ON THE PRESENT VOLUME

Cuneiform Text

As in previous volumes, the cuneiform text has been generated automatically from the composite transliteration provided by the author, using programs and fonts created by the SAA Project. In response to feedback received from users of the previous volumes, the font chosen for printing the cuneiform text is again the same as in SAACT 1–3, while the somewhat more sophisticated font used in SAACT 4–7 is here used in the sign list only.

Black characters stand for text preserved in at least one manuscript while white characters stand for restored text and correspond to items within square brackets in the transliteration. Note that portions of text restorable from refrains and parallels but not actually extant in any manuscript are also given in white characters. Unrestorable portions of the text are indicated by shaded areas.

The sign list contains all the syllabic and logographic sign values occurring in the composite text and their frequencies. The sign numbers given in boldface are those of R. Borger's *Assyrisch-babylonische Zeichenliste* with some minor modifications. It should be bore in mind that the indication of broken signs is not intended to render the cuneiform text more "scientific" since the representations are for the most part merely stylized and symbolic. No attempt has been made to provide a wedge by wedge reconstruction of the preserved portions of signs. The primary purpose of the cuneiform text here is pedagogical (either for classroom use or for self-study). Research on the cuneiform text itself must be done on the basis of the original text publications or the original tablets. The cuneiform text provided here is not suited for that purpose. Furthermore, the text, being a composite from numerous fragments, certainly does not represent any ancient text that would have existed as such.

Transliteration

The composite text in this volume has been established on the basis a *Partitur* collating line by line all the known manuscripts, both published and unpublished. However, the *Partitur* as such is not included in this monograph. It will be published together with hand copies of new materials and collations of already published manuscripts in my forthcoming book. Significant text variants are noted in the philological notes, but other minor variations, such as mere orthographical variants, are not provided in this edition and are reserved for the forthcoming critical edition of the *Babylonian Theodicy* and its ancient commentary.

Translation

In keeping with the aims of the series in which this text is being published, the translation offered here is intended primarily for students of Assyriology, who will use it in conjunction with the Akkadian text also published here. However, because the *Babylonian Theodicy* may be of interest to biblical scholars and other students of ancient Near Eastern religion, some observations about this translation are needed for those who cannot relate it to the original text.

Any attempt to translate ancient poetry into English represents a compromise between being faithful to the original text and meeting the demands of readable English. In particular, a readable English translation can seldom and then only imperfectly reflect either the word order or the specific grammatical and syntactical structures of the original Akkadian text.

The interpretation of the *Babylonian Theodicy* is particularly difficult, especially because its author, Saggil-kīnam-ubbib, often departed from conventional Akkadian word order and altered case endings for the sake of the acrostic and the rhymes. Its highly poetic style, its rare words, and its many metaphors pose additional problems in rendering the text into English. In some cases, a literal translation simply makes little or no good sense. In such cases, I attempt to offer a translation that conveys not only the literal meaning of each phrase but also an interpretation of the general idea behind it. Such interpretive translations are normally set in italics to call the reader's attention to them. When, however, my interpretation differs significantly from the literal wording, I have noted the literal rendering either by a parenthesis in the text or by an explicit explanation in the philological notes.

To properly understand the translation, the following points should be noted:

- When parts of a word or line in the original text are missing or illegible, this will normally be indicated in the translation by inserting a dot for each missing sign. However, when the missing portion of the text can be reconstructed with sufficient probability, a translation of the reconstructed portion is put in square brackets. If only a part of an Akkadian word needs to be reconstructed, e.g. the initial or final syllables, this will be indicated optically by bracketing a corresponding portion of the English word used to translate it, even though there is obviously no semantic correspondence between the syllables of the Akkadian and the syllables of the English terms.
- When the reconstruction of an Akkadian word is questionable, a superscript question mark is placed behind the English term used to translate it, e.g. *t[urn back*$^{?}$].
- When, for the sake of English grammar and style, words having no direct correspondent in the Akkadian text must be inserted into the translation they are usually set off in parentheses. This is not done, however, when the insertion is self-evident.
- Parentheses are also used to insert explanations and clarifications into the text, namely "(i.e.: ...)" to explain the exact meaning of an unclear term or phrase and "(lit.: "...") to identify a term or phrase whose normal "dictionary" meaning makes little or no sense in context and thus demands an interpreta-

tion. Since every translation is simultaneously an interpretation, the boundaries between the literal meaning and its interpretation are always rather fluid. Thus only in the more egregious instances will attention be called to such differences in this manner.

- The Akkadian text has neither definite nor indefinite articles, whereas the English translation often requires that these be inserted to clarify the reference of a noun. In most cases, there is no need to call attention to such insertions, but in cases where the use or omission of an article can significantly change the meaning of a term or phrase, the respective article is always written in parentheses. This is especially the case in connection with the words "god" and "goddess" as translations of *ilu* and *ištar*/*iltu*. As noted above, pp xlvii–xlviii, these terms can be read as concrete terms in the sense of "*A* god/goddess" or "*THE* god/goddess". But without further qualification they can also be interpreted to mean something abstract like "deity / she-deity". For this reason, whenever an article must be inserted before "god" or "goddess" for the sake of English style, it will be set in parentheses.
- In passages where the Akkadian text uses only the simple past tense, English grammar often requires distinguishing between the simple past, the perfect, the continuous perfect, and the past perfect. Because these modifications are so frequent, I do not normally call attention to them.

Glossary and Indices

The glossary was prepared by the SAA Project staff from the transliteration. The glossary contains all the lexically identifiable words occurring in the composite text. Forms that occur only in the variants and words attested only in the *Theodicy Commentary* are not included in the glossary or other indices. The list of logograms has been computer generated from the transliteration.

MANUSCRIPTS

MS A: BM 34633: col i = 28–45; col ii–iii = traces; col iv = 279–297 (LAMBERT 1960, pls. 19 and 25)

MS B: BM 34773: col i = 3–34; col ii = traces; col iii 193–201; col iv 262–297 (LAMBERT 1960, pls. 19 and 24)

MS C: BM 35405: obv = 18–57; rev = traces (LAMBERT 1960, pl. 20)

MS D: BM 40098+40124+77225[179]: col i 55–66; col ii = 120–136; col iii = 139–156; col iv = 210–227 (Oshima, forthcoming; BM 40098 = LAMBERT 1960, pls. 21 and 23; BM 40124 = LAMBERT 1960, pl. 20)

MS E: BM 47745: obv = 72–85; rev = 203–213 (Oshima, forthcoming)

MS F: BM 68589: obv = 46–66; rev = 224–240 (Oshima, forthcoming)

MS G: K 1743+10858 (+) K 3452+5457+8463+10301+17578+17861+18535+20280+Sm 147 + 624 (+) K 5932 (+) K 8491+13929 (Oshima, forthcoming)[180]

MS G1: K 1743+10858: 193–210 (Oshima, forthcoming; LAMBERT 1960, pl. 22)

MS G2: K 3452+5457+17578+Sm 147: col i 34–57; col iv 258–289 (Oshima, forthcoming; K 3452+Sm 147 = LAMBERT 1960, pls. 20 and 25)

MS G3: K 5932: 179–189 (Oshima, forthcoming; LAMBERT 1960, pl. 22)

MS G4: K 8463+10301+20280: col i = 1–17; col ii = 79–88; col iii = 229–236 (Oshima, forthcoming; K 8463 = LAMBERT 1960, pls. 19 and 23; K 10301 =*ibid.*, pl. 19)

MS G5: K 8491+13929: col i = 69–78; col iii = 158–169; col iv 237–239 (Oshima, forthcoming; LAMBERT 1960, pls. 21-22)

MS G6: K 17861+18535+Sm 624: col iv = 250–259 (Oshima, forthcoming)

MS H: K 9290+9297: col i = 48–80; col ii 125–143; col iii = 176–191; col iv = 235–269 (LAMBERT 1960, pls. 21–22)

MS I: VAT 10567: 185–255 (LAMBERT 1960, pl. 23)

---

179 BM 77225 was identified as a join of BM 40124 by I. Finkel. Lambert (1960, p. 69) has already suspected that BM 40124 and 40098 might be joins.

180 Lambert has already noted that his MSs B (K 8463) and E (K 8491+13929) belong to the same tablet, *ibid*.

BIBLIOGRAPHY[181]

ABUSCH, Tz.
1987 "*Alaktu* and *Halakhah*: Oracular Decision, Divine Revelation," *Harvard Theological Review* 80. 15–42.

ALBERTZ, R.
1981 "Der sozialgeschichtliche Hintergrund des Hiobbuches und der »Babylonischen Theodizee«," in JEREMIAS und PERLITT eds., *Die Botschaft und die Boten: Festschrift für Hans Walter Wolff zum 70. Geburtstag*. Neukirchener. pp. 349–72.

ALBREKTSON, B.
1967 *History and the Gods: An Essay on the Idea of Historical Events as Divine Manifestations in the Ancient Near East and in Israel*. Coniectanea Biblica Old Testament Series 1. Lund.

ALSTER, B.
1997 *Proverbs of Ancient Sumer: The World's Earliest Proverb Collections*, vol. I and II. Bethesda.
2005 *Wisdom of Ancient Sumer*. Bethesda.

AL-RAWI, F. N. H.
2008 "Inscriptions from the Tombs of the Queens of Assyria," in Curtis *et al.* eds., *New Light on Nimrud: Proceedings of the Nimrud Conference 11th–13th March 2002*. London. 119–38.

AL-RAWI, F. N. H. and GEROGE, A. R.
2006 "Tablets from the Sippar Library XIII: *Enūma Anu Enlil* XX," *Iraq* 68. 23–57.

ANNUS, A. and LENZI, A.
2011 Ludlul bēl nēmeqi: *The Standard Babylonian Poem of the Righteous Sufferer*. State Archives of Assryia Cuneiform Texts vol. 7. Helsinki.

ARNAUD, D.
1972 "Deux *Kudurru* de Larsa: II étude épigraphique," *RA* 66. 163–76.

BEAULIEU, P.-A.
1992 "New Light on Secret Knowledge in Late Babylonian Culture," *ZA* 82. 98–111.
2000 "The Descendants of Sîn-lēqi-unninni," in MARZAHN and NEUMANN eds., *Assyriologica et Semitica: Festschrift für Joachim Oelsner, anläßlich seines 65. Geburtstages am 18. Februar 1997*. AOAT 252. Münster. 1–16.
2007 "The Social and Intellectual Setting of Babylonian Wisdom Literature," in CLIFFORD ed., *Wisdom Literature in Mesopotamia and Israel*. SBL Symposium Series 36. Atlanta. 3–19.

BECKMAN, G.
2002 "'My Sun-God': Reflections of Mesopotamian Conceptions of Kingship among the Hittites," in PANAINO and PETTINATO eds., *Ideologies as Intercultural Phenomena: Melammu Symposia* III. Milano. 37–43.

[181] Regarding the abbreviations, I basically follow the abbreviation system of the *Chicago Assyrian Dictionary*.

BIGGS, R. T.
1969 "Akkadian Didactic and Wisdom Literature," in PRITCHARD ed., *Ancient Near Eastern Texts Relating to the Old Testament*, 3rd ed. with supplement. Princeton. 592–607.

BÖCK, B.
2000 *Die babylonisch-assyrische Morphoskopie*. *AfO* B 27. Wien.

BORGER, R.
1974 "Die Beschwörungsserie *BĪT MĒSERI* und die Himmelfahrt Henochs," *JNES* 33. 183–96.

BOTTÉRO, J.
1977 "Le problème du mal en mesopotamie ancienne: Prologue à une étude du 'Juste Souffrant'," *Recherches et Documents du Centre Thomas More*, Document 77/7, no. 15. 1–43.

BRINKMAN, J.A.
1968 *A Political History of Post-Kassite Babylonia 1158–772 B.C.* AnOr 43. Rome.
1974 "The Monarchy in the Time of the Kassite Dynasty," in GARELLI ed., *Le Palais et la royauté* (Archéologie et Civilisation), *XIXe Rencontre Assyriologique Internationale*. Paris. 395–408.

BUCCELLATI, G.
1972 "Tre Saggi Sulla Sapenza Mesopotamica," *Oriens Antiquus* 11. 1–36 and 161–78.
1981 "Wisdom and Not: The Case of Mesopotamia," *JAOS* 101. 35–47.

BURKERT, W.
1995 "Der Geheime Reiz des Verborgenen: Antike Mysterienkulte," in KIPPENBERG and STROUMSA eds., *Secrecy and Concealment: Studies in the History of Mediterranean and Near Eastern Religions*. Studies in the History of Religions: *Numen* Book Series LXV. Leiden/New York/Köln. 79–100.

BUTLER, S. A. L.
1998 *Mesopotamian Conceptions of Dreams and Dream Rituals*. AOAT 258. Münster.

CAVIGNEAUX, A.
2005 "Shulgi, Nabonide, et le Grecs," in SEFATI *et al.* eds, "*An Experienced Scribe Who Neglects Nothing*:" *Ancient Near Eastern Studies in Honor of Jacob Klein*. Bethesda. 2005. 63–72.

CHARPIN, D. (translated by J. M. TODD)
2010 *Reading and Writing in Babylon*. Cambridge/London.

CUNNINGHAM, G.
2007 "*Deliver Me from Evil*": *Mesopotamian Incantations 2500–1500 BC*. Studia Pohl: Series Maior, Dissertationes scientificae de Rebus Orientis Antiqui 17. Rome.

DENNING-BOLLE, S. J.
1987 "Wisdom and Dialogue in the Ancient Near East," *Numen* 34. 214–34.
1992 *Wisdom in Akkadian Literature: Expression, Instruction, Dialogue*. Leiden.

VAN DIJK, J. J.
1962 UVB 18, see LENZEN *et. al.*

VAN DIJK, J. and MAYER, W. R.
1980 *Texte aus dem Rēš-Heiligtum in Uruk-Warka*. Bagh. Mitt. Beiheft 2. Berlin.

EBELING, E.
1924 "Ein babylonischer Kohelet," *BBK* I/1. Berlin.

FARBER, W.
2007 "Lamaštu — Agent of a Specific Disease or a Generic Destroyer of Health?" in FINKEL and GELLER eds., *Disease in Babylonia*. Cuneiform Monograph 36. Leiden/Boston. 137–45.

FINKEL, I. L.
1988 "Adad-apla-iddina, Esagil-kīn-apli, and the Series SA.GIG," in LEICHTY, DE J. ELLIS, and GERARDI eds., *A Scientific Humanist: Studies in Memory of Abraham Sachs*. Philadelphia. 143–59.
2000 "On Late Babylonian Medical Training," in GEORGE and FINKEL eds., *Wisdom, Gods and Literature: Studies in Assyriology in Honour of W. G. Lambert*. Winona Lake. 137–223.

FOSTER, B. R.
2005 *Before the Muses: An Anthology of Akkadian Literature*, 3rd Edition. Bethesda.
2007 *Akkadian Literature of the Late Period*. Guides to the Mesopotamian Textual Record 2. Münster.

FRAHM, E.
2011 *Babylonian and Assyrian Text Commentaries: Origins of Interpretation*. Guides to the Mesopotamian Textual Record 5. Münster.

GALTER, H.
1983 *Der Gott Ea/Enki in der akkadischen Überlieferung: Eine Bestandsaufnahme des vorhandenen Materials*. Graz. (Graz University Dissertation.)

GELLER, M. J.
2000 "Incipits and Rubrics," in GEORGE and FINKEL eds., *Wisdom, Gods and Literature: Studies in Assyriology in Honour of W. G. Lambert*. Winona Lake. 225–58.
2007 *Evil Demons: Canonical* Utukkū Lemnūtu *Incantations*. SAACT 5. Helsinki.
2010 *Ancient Babylonian Medicine: Theory and Practice*. Chichester.

GEORGE, A. R.
1993 *House Most High: The Temples of Ancient Mesopotamia*. Winona Lake.
2003 *The Babylonian Gilgamesh Epic: Introduction, Critical Edition and Cuneiform Texts*. Oxford.

GESCHE, P. D.
2001 *Schulunterricht in Babylonien im ersten Jahrtausend v. Chr*. AOAT 275. Münster.

GOODNICK-WESTENHOLZ, J.
2004 "The Good Shepherd," in PANAINO and PIRAS eds., *Melammu Symposia* IV: *Schools of Oriental Studies and the Development of Modern Historiography*. Milano. 281–310.

GRONEBERG, B. R. M.
1996 "Towards a Definition of Literariness as Applied to Akkadian Literature," in VOGELZANG and VANSTIPHOUT eds., *Mesopotamian Poetic Language: Sumerian and Akkadian*. Cuneiform Monograph 6. Groningen. 59–84.

1997 *Lob der Ištar: Gebet und Ritual an die altbabylonische Venusgöttin*, tanatti ištar. Cuneiform Monograph 8. Groningen.

HEEBEL, N. P.
2010 "Neues von Esagil-kīn-apli: Die ältere Version der physiognomischen Omenserie *alamdimmû*," in MAUL and HEEBEL, eds., *Assur-Forschungen: Arbeiten aus der Forschungsstelle »Edition literarischer Keilschrifttexte aus Assur« der Heidelberger Akademie der Wissenschaften*. Wiesbaden. 139–87.

HOROWITZ, W. and WATSON, P. J.
1991 "Further Notes on Birmingham Cuneiform Tablets Volume 1," *Acta Sumerologica* 13. 409–17.

HRŮŠA, I.
2010 *Die akkadische Synonymenliste*, Malku = Šarru: *Eine Textedition mit Übersetzung und Kommentar*. AOAT 50. Münster.

HUNGER, H.
1968 *Babylonische und assyrische Kolophone*. AOAT 2. Kevelaer/ Neukirchen-Vluyn.
1976 *Spätbabylonische Texte aus Uruk*, Teil I. Ausgrabungen der Deutschen Forschungsgemeinschaft in Uruk-Warka, Bd. 9. Berlin.
1987 "Empfehlungen an den König," ROCHBERG-HALTON, ed., *Language, Literature, and History: Philological and Historical Studies Presented to Erica Reiner*. American Oriental Series 67. New Haven, 157–66.

HUROWITZ, V. A.
2004 "^{d}Narru and ^{d}Zulummar in the Babylonian Theodicy (*BWL* 88: 276–77)," *JAOS* 124, 777–78.
2008 "Tales of Two Sages — Towards and Image of the "Wise Man" in Akkadian Writings," in PERDUE ed., *Scribes, Sages, and Seers: The Sage in the Eastern Mediterranean World*. Göttingen. 64–94.
2010 "Name *Midrashim* and Word Plays on Names in Akkadian Historical Writings," in HOROWITZ, GABBAY, and VUKOSAVOVIĆ eds., *A Woman of Valor: Jerusalem Ancient Near Eastern Studies in Honor of Joan Goodnick Westenholz*. Biblioteca del Próximo Oriente Antiguo 8. Madrid. 87–104.

IZRE'EL, SH.
1992 "The Study of Oral Poetry: Reflections of a Neophyte: Can We Learn Anything on Orality from the Study of Akkadian Poetry, Especially in Akhetaton?" in VOGELZANG and VANSTIPHOUT eds., *Mesopotamian Epic Literature: Oral or Aural?* Lewiston/Queenston/ Lamperter. 155–225.
1996 "Mesopotamian Literature in Contemporary Setting: Translating Akkadian Myths," in VOGELZANG and VANSTIPHOUT eds., *Mesopotamian Poetic Language: Sumerian and Akkadian*. Cuneiform Monograph 6. Groningen. 85–125.

JACOBSEN, TH.
1976 *The Treasures of Darkness: A History of Mesopotamian Religion*. New Haven.

JEAN, C.
2006 *La magie néo-assyrienne en contexte: Recherches sur le métier d'exorciste et le concept d'*āšipūtu. SAAS 17. Helsinki.

JURSA, M.
1999 *Das Archiv des Bēl-Rēmanni*. Istanbul.
2005 *Neo-Babylonian Legal and Administrative Document: Typological, Contents and Archives*. Guides to the Mesopotamian Textual Record 1. Münster.

KATZ, D.
2003 *The Image of the Netherworld in the Sumerian Sources*. Bethesda.

KLEIN, J.
1981 *The Royal Hymns of Shulgi, King of Ur: Man's Quest for Immortal Fame*. Philadelphia.

KREBERNIK, M.
2003–04 "Altbabylonische Hymnen an die Muttergöttin (HS 1884)," *AfO* 50. 11–20.

KREBERNIK, M. and STRECK, M. P.
2001 "*šumman lā qabi'āt ana balaṭim* ... Wärst du nicht zum Leben berufen ...: Der Irrealis im Altbabylonischen," in BARTELMUS and NEBES eds., *Sachverhalt und Zeitbezug: Semitistische und alttestamentaliche Studien: Adolf Denz zum 65. Geburtstag*. Jenaer Beiträge zum Vorderen Orient 4. Wiesbaden. 51–78.

LABAT, R.
1970 *Les religions du Proche-Orient asiatique: Textes babyloniens, ougaritiques, hittites*. Paris.

LAMBERT, W.G.
1957 "Ancestors, Authors, and Canonicity," *JCS* 11. 1–14.
1960 *Babylonian Wisdom Literature*. Oxford.
1962 "A Catalogue of Texts and Authors," *JCS* 16. 59–77.
1967 "The Gula Hymn of Bulluṭsa-rabi," *OrNS* 36. 105–32 with pls. VIII–XXIII.
1970 "Objects Inscribed and Uninscribed," *AfO* 23. 46–51.
1980 "The Theology of Death," in ALSTER ed., *Death in Mesopotamia: Papers Read at the XXXVIe Rencontre assyriologique internationale*. Mesopotamia Copenhagen Studies in Assyriology 8. Copenhagen. 53-66.
1987 "A Further Attempt at the Babylonian 'Man and His God'," in ROCHBERG-HALTON ed., *Language, Literature, and History: Philological and Historical Studies Presented to Erica Reiner*. New Haven. 187–202.
1995 "Some New Babylonian Wisdom Literature," in DAY *et al.* eds., *Wisdom in Ancient Israel: Essays in Honour of J. A. Emerton*. Cambridge/New York. 30–42.

LANDSBERGER, B.
1936 "Die babylonische Theodizee (akrostichisches Zwiegespräch; sog. "Kohelet")," *ZA* 43. 32–76.

LEICHTY, E.
2011 *The Royal Inscriptions of Esarhaddon, King of Assyria (680–669 BC)*. The Royal Inscriptions of the Neo-Assyrian Period 4. Winona Lake.

LENZEN, H. J. with V. HALLER, A., DIJK, J. J. and STROMMENGER, E.
1962 *XVIII. vorläufiger Bericht über die von dem Deutschen Archäologischen Institut und der Deutschen Orient-Gesellschaft aus Mitteln der Deutschen Forschungsgemeinschaft unternommenen Ausgrabungen in Uruk-Warka: Winter 1959/60*. Berlin.

LENZI, A.
2008 *Secrecy and the Gods: Secret Knowledge in Ancient Mesopotamia and Biblica Israel*. SAAS 19. Helsinki.

LIMET, H.
1971 *Les légendes des sceaux cassites*. Brussel.

LITKE, R. L.
1998 *A Reconstruction of the Assyro-Babylonian God-Lists*, AN:^{d}A-NU-UM *and* AN: ANU ŠÁ AMĒLI. New Haven.

LIVINGSTONE, A.
2007 "Ashurbanipal: Literate or Not?" *ZA* 97. 98–118.

LUCKENBILL, D. D.
1924 *The Annals of Sennacherib*. OIP 2. Chicago.

LUUKKO, M.
2007 "The Administrative Roles of the "Chief Scribe" and the "Palace Scribe" in the Neo-Assyrian Period," *State Archives of Assyria Bulletin* 16. 227–56.

MACGINNIS, J. D. A.
2002 "The Use of Writing Boards in the Neo-Babylonian Temple Administration at Sippar," *Iraq* 64. 217–36.

MATTINGLY, G. L.
1990 "The Pious Sufferer: Mesopotamia's Traditional Theodicy and Job's Counselors," in HALLO, JONES, and MATTINGLY eds., *The Bible in the Light of Cuneiform Literature: Scripture in Context* III. Lewiston/Queenston/Lamperter. 305–48.

MAUL, S. M.
1994 *Zukunftsbewältigung: Eine Untersuchung altorientalischen Denkens anhand der babylonisch-assyrischen Löserituale* (Namburbi). Baghdader Forschungen 18. Mainz.
2010 "Die Tontafelbibliothek aus dem sogenannten »Haus des Beschwörungspriesters«," in MAUL and HEEßEL, eds., *Assur-Forschungen: Arbeiten aus der Forschungsstelle »Edition literarischer Keilschrifttexte aus Assur« der Heidelberger Akademie der Wissenschaften*. Wiesbaden. 189–228.

MAYER, W. R.
1976 *Untersuchungen zur Formensprache der babylonischen "Gebetsbeschwörungen"*. Rome.
1993 "Das Ritual *BMS* 12 mit dem Gebet "Marduk 5"," *OrNS* 62. 313–37.

MEIER, G.
1937–39 "Kommentare aus dem Archiv der Tempelschule in Assur," *AfO* 12. 237–46.
1942 "Ein Kommentar zu einer Sebstprädikation des Marduk aus Assur," *ZA* 47. 241–46.

MICHALOWSKI, P.
1977 "The Death of Šulgi," *OrNS* 46. 220–25.
1987 "Charisma and Control: On Continuity and Change in Early Mesopotamian Bureaucratic Systems," in GIBSON and BIGGS eds., *The Organization of Power: Aspects of Bureaucracy in the Ancient Near East*. Studies in Ancient Oriental Civilization 46. Chicago. 45–57.

MITTERMAYER, C.
2009 *Enmerkara und der Herr von Arata: Ein ungleicher Wettstreit*. Orbis Biblicus et Orientalis 239. Fribourg/Göttingen.

OELSNER, J.
1986 *Materialien zur babylonischen Gesellschaft und Kultur in hellenistischer Zeit*. Assyriologia VII. Budapest.

OSHIMA, T.
2006 "Marduk, the Canal Digger," *JANES* 30. 77–88.
2011 *Babylonian Prayers to Marduk*. Orientalische Religionen in der Antike 7. Tübingen.

PARPOLA, S.
1970 *Letters from Assyrian Scholars to the Kings Esarhaddon and Assurbanipal*, Pt I: Text. AOAT 5/1. Kevelaer/Nuekirchen-Vluyn.
1983 *Letters from Assyrian Scholars to the Kings Esarhaddon and Assurbanipal*, Pt II: Commentary and Appendices. AOAT 5/2. Kevelaer/Nuekirchen-Vluyn.
1995 "The Assyrian Cabinet," in DIETRICH and LORETZ eds., *Vom Alten Orient zum Alten Testament: Festschrift für Wolfram Freiherrn von Soden zum 85. Geburtstag am 19. Juni 1993*. AOAT 240. Kevelaer/Neukirchen–Vluyn. 379–401.

PEČÍRKOVÁ, J.
1985 "Divination and Politics in the Late Assyrian Empire," *ArOr* 53. 155–68.

PEDERSÉN, O.
1986 *Archives and Libraries in the City of Assur: A Survey of the Material from the German Excavations*, Pt. 2. Acta Universitatis Upsaliensis Studia Semitica Upsaliensia 8. Uppsala.

POMPONIO, F.
1978 *Nabû: il culto e la figura di un dio del Pantheon babilonese ed assiro*. Studi Semitici 51. Rome.

PONCHIA, S.
1996 *La palma e il tamarisco: e altri dialoghi mesopotamici*. Venice.

PONGRATZ-LEISTEN, B.
1999 *Herrschaftswissen in Mesopotamien: Formen der Kommunikation zwischen Gott und König im 2. und 1. Jahrtausend v.Chr*. SAAS 10. Helsinki.

POPE, M. H.
1974 *Job: Introduction, Translation, and Notes*. 3rd ed. The Anchor Bible 15. Garden City.

RADNER, K.
2009 "The Assyrian King and his Scholars: The Syrio-Anatolian and the Egyptian Schools," in LUUKKO, SVÄRD, and MATTILA eds., *Of God(s), Trees, Kings, and Scholars: Neo-Assyrian and Related Studies in Honour of Simo Parpola*. Helsinki. 221–306.

REINER, E.
1961 "The Etiological Myth of the "Seven Sages"," *OrNS* 30. 1–11.
1985 *Your Thwarts in Pieces, Your Mooring Rope Cut: Poetry from Babylonia and Assyria*. Michigan.

RENGER, J.
1969 "Untersuchungen zum Priestertum in der altbabylonischen, Zeit 2. Teil," *ZA* 59. 104–230.

ROCHBERG, F.
2000 "Scribes and Scholars: The *ṭupšar Enūma Anu Enlil*," in MARZAHN and NEUMANN eds., *Assyriologica et Semitica: Festschrift für Joachim Oelsner anläßlich seines 65. Geburtstages am 18. Februar 1997*. AOAT 252. Münster. 359–75.

ROTH, M. T.
1995 *Law Collections from Mesopotamia and Asia Minor*. Atlanta.

SALLABERGER, W.
2002 "Den Göttern nahe — und fern den Menschen? Formen der Sakralität des altmesopotamischen Herrschers," in ERKENS ed., *Die Sakralität von Herrschaft: Herrschaftslegitimierung im Wechsel der Zeiten und Räume. Fünfzehn interdisziplinäre Beiträge zu einem weltweiten und epochenübergreifenden Phänomen*. Berlin. 85–98.

SCHAUDIG, H.
2012 "Erlärungsmuster von Katastrophen im Alten Orient," in BERLEJUNG ed., *Disaster and Relief Management: Katastrophen und ihre Bewältigung*. Tübingen. 425–43.

SCHWEMER, D.
2010 "Fighting Witchcraft before the Moon and Sun: a Therapeutic Ritual from Neo-Babylonian Sippar," *OrNS* 79. 480–504.

SELZ, G. J.
2000 "Der sogenannte 'geflügelte Tempel' und die 'Himmelfahrt' der Herrscher. Spekulationen über ein ungelöstes Problem der altakkadischen Glyptik und dessen möglichen rituellen Hintergrung," in GRAZIANI ed., *Studi sul Vicino Oriente Antico dedicati alla memoria di Luigi Cagni*, vol. II. Napoli. 962–83.
2001 ""Guter Hirte, Wiser Fürst" — Zur Vorstellung von Macht und zur Macht der Vorstellung im altmesopotamischen Herrschaftsparadigma," *AoF* 28. 8–39.
2002 ""Streit herrscht, Gewalt droht" — Zu Konfliktregelung und Recht in der frühdynastischen und altakkadischen Zeit," *WZKM* 92. 155–203.
2008 "The Divine Prototypes," in BRISCH ed., *Religion and Power: Divine Kingship in the Ancient World and Beyond*. Oriental Institute Seminars 4. Chicago. 13–31.
2010 ""The Poor Are the Silent Ones in the Country:" On the Loss of Legitimacy; Challenging Power in Early Mesopotamia," in CHARVÁT and MAŘIKOVÁ VLČKOVÁ eds., *Who Was King? Who Was Not King?: The Rulers and the Ruled in the Ancient Near East*. Prague. 1–15.

SEUX, M.-J.
1967 *Épithètes Royales Akkadiennes et Sumériennes*. Paris.

SITZLER, D.
1995 "*Vorwurf gegen Gott*": *Ein religiöses Motiv im Alten Orient* (*Ägypten und Mesopotamien*). Studies in Oriental Religions 32. Wiesbaden.

SJÖBERG, Å. W.
1972 "Die göttliche Abstammung der sumerisch-babylonischen Herrscher," *Orientalia Suecana* 21. 87–112.

VON SODEN, W. F.
1956 "Zum akkadischen Wörterbuch. 81–87," *OrNS* 25. 241–50.
1957 "Zu einigen altbabylonischen Dichtungen," *OrNS* 26. 306–20.
1965 "Das Fragen nach der Gerechtigkeit Gottes im alten Orient," *MDOG* 96. 41–59.
1974–7 "Zwei Königsgebete an Ištar aus Assyrien," *AfO* 25. 37–49.
1981 "Untersuchungen zur babylonischen Metrik, Teil I," *ZA* 71. 161–204.
1984 "Untersuchungen zur babylonischen Metrik, Teil II," *ZA* 74. 213–34.

1990 "»Weisheitstexte« in akkadischer Sprache," in *Texte aus der Umwelt des Alten Testaments Band III, Weisheitstexte, Mythen und Epen: Weisheitstexte* I. Gütersloh. 110–88.

SOLL, W. M.
1988 "Babylonian and Biblical Acrostics," *Bib.* 69. 305–23.

SPIECKERMANN, H.
1998 "*Ludlul bēl nēmeqi* und die Frage nach der Gerechtigkeit Gottes," in MAUL ed., *Festschrift für Rykle Borger*. Cuneiform Monograph 10. Groningen. 329–41.

STAMM, J. J.
1939 *Die akkadische Namengebung*. MVAG 44. Leipzig.
1944 "Die Theodizee in Babylon und Israel," *JEOL* 9. 99–107.

STEINKELLER, P.
1999 "On Rulers, Priests and Sacred Marriage: Tracing the Evolution of Early Sumerian Kingship," in WATANABE ed., *Priests and Officials in the Ancient Near East: Papers of the Second Colloquium on the Ancient Near East – The City and its Life held at the Middle Eastern Culture Centre in Japan (Mitaka, Tokyo), March 22–24, 1996*. Heidelberg. 103–37.

STOL, M.
1996 "The Reversibility of Human Fate in Ludlul II," in TUNCA and DEHESELLE, eds., *Tablettes et images aux pays de sumer et d'akkad: Mélanges offerts à Monsieur H. Limet*. Liège. 179–83.
2000 *Birth in Babylonia and the Bible: Its Mediterranean Setting*. Cuneiform Monograph 14. Groningen.

STRECK, M. P.
1999 *Die Bildersprache der akkadischen Epik*. AOAT 264. Münster.

ŠAŠKOVÁ, K.
2010 "Adad-šumu-uṣur and his Family in the Service of Assyrian Kings," in CHARVÁT and MAŘIKOVÁ VLČKOVÁ eds., *Who Was King? Who Was Not King?: The Rulers and the Ruled in the Ancient Near East*. Prague. 113–30.

VAN DER TOORN, K.
1991 "The Ancient Near Eastern Literary Dialogue as a Vehicle of Critical Reflection," in REININK and VANSTIPHOUT eds., *Dispute Poems and Dialogues in the Ancient and Mediaeval Near East: Forms and Types of Literary Debates in Semitic and Related Literatures*. OLA 42. Leuven. 59–75.
2003 "Theodicy in Akkadian Literature," in LAATO and DE MOOR eds., *Theodicy in the World of the Bible*. Leiden/Boston. 57–89.
2007 "Why Wisdom Became a Secret: On Wisdom as a Written Genre," in CLIFFORD ed., *Wisdom Literature in Mesopotamia and Israel*. SBL Symposium Series 36. Atlanta. 21–9.

UEHLINGER, C.
1997 "Qohelet im Horizont mesopotamischer, levantinischer und ägyptischer Weisheitsliteratur der persischen und hellenistischen Zeit," in SCHWIENHORST-SCHÖNBERGER ed., *Das Buch Kohelet: Studien zur Struktur, Geschichte, Rezeption und Theologie*. Berlin/New York. 156–247.
2007 "Das Hiob-Buch im Kontext der altorientalischen Literatur- und Religionsgeschichte," in KRÜGER *et al.* eds., *Das Buch Hiob und seine Interpretationen: Beiträge zum Hiob-Symposium auf dem Monte Verità vom 14.–19. August 2005*. Abhandlungen zur Theologie des Alten und Neuen Testaments 88. Zürich. 97–163.

UNGNAD, A.
1941–44 "Besprechungskunst und Astrologie in Babylonien," *AfO* 14. 251–84.

VANSTIPHOUT, H. L. J.
1990 "The Mesopotamian Debate Poems: A General Presentation (Part I)," *Acta Sumerologica* 12. 271–318.
1991 "Lore, Learning, and Levity in the Sumerian Disputations: A Matter of Form, or Substance?" in REININK and VANSTIPHOUT eds., *Dispute Poems and Dialogues in the Ancient and Mediaeval Near East: Forms and Types of Literary Debates in Semitic and Related Literatures*. OLA 42. Leuven. 23–46.
1992 "The Mesopotamian Debate Poems: A General Presentation. Part II: The Subject," *Acta Sumerologica* 14. 339–67.

VELDHUIS, N.
1997 *Elementary Education at Nippur: The Lists of Trees and Wooden Objects*. Groningen PhD Thesis. 1997.
2004 *Religion, Literature, and Scholarship: The Sumerian Composition Nanše and the Birds, with a Catalogue of Sumerian Bird Names*. Cuneiform Monographs 22. Leiden/Boston.

VOGELZANG, M. E.
1991 "Some Questions about the Akkadian Disputes," in REININK and VANSTIPHOUT eds., *Dispute Poems and Dialogues in the Ancient and Mediaeval Near East: Forms and Types of Literary Debates in Semitic and Related Literatures*. OLA 42. Leuven. 47–57.

VOLK, K.
2011 "Über Bilding und Ausbildung in Babylonien am Anfang des 2. Jahrtausends v. Chr.," *OrNS* 80. 269–99.

WASSERMAN, N.
2002 "The Modal Particle *tuša* in Old-Babylonian: A Syntatic and Semantic Synopsis," *NABU* 2002, no. 47.

WEIDNER, E.
1941–4 "Die astrologische Serie Enûma Anu Enlil," *AfO* 14. 172–95; 308–18.
1959–60 "Ein «Kommentar» zu *šumma izbu* Tafel VI," *AfO* 19. 151–52.

VON WEIHER, E.
1983 *Spätbabylonische Texte aus Uruk*, Teil II. Ausgrabungen der Deutschen Forschungsgemeinschaft in Uruk-Warka, Bd. 10. Berlin.
1988 *Spätbabylonische Texte aus Uruk*, Teil III. Ausgrabungen der Deutschen Forschungsgemeinschaft in Uruk-Warka, Bd. 12. Berlin.
1993 *Uruk: Spätbabylonische Texte aus dem Planquadrat U 18*, Teil IV. Ausgrabungen in Uruk-Warka 12. Mainz.
1998 *Uruk: Spätbabylonische Texte aus dem Planquadrat U 18*, Teil V. Ausgrabungen in Uruk-Warka 13. Mainz.

WILCKE, C.
1982 Review of H. Hunger, *Spätbabylonische Texte aus Uruk*, Teil I. Berlin. 1976. *BiOr* 39. 141–45.
1988 "König Šulgis Himmelfahrt," RAUNIG and LAUBSCHER eds., *Festschrift László Vajda: Münchner Beiträge zur Völkerkunde*. München. 245–55.

2002 "Vom göttlichen Wesen des Königtums und seinem Ursprung im Himmel," in ERKENS ed., *Die Sakralität von Herrschaft: Herrschaftslegitimierung im Wechsel der Zeiten und Räume*. Berlin. 63–83.

WUNSCH, C.
2003–4 "Findelkinder und Adoption nach neubabylonischen Quellen," *AfO* 50. 174–268.

ZAMAZALOVÁ, S.
2011 "The Education of Neo-Assyrian Princes," in RADNER and ROBSON eds., *The Oxford Handbook of Cuneiform Culture*. Oxford. 312–30.

ZGOLL, A.
2003 *Die Kunst des Betens: Form und Funktion, Theologie und Psychagogik in babylonisch-assyrischen Handerhebungsgebeten an Ištar*. AOAT 308. Münster.

ZIMMERN, H.
1895 "Weiteres zur babylonischen Metrik," *ZA* 10. 1–24.

CUNEIFORM TEXT

The Babylonian Theodicy

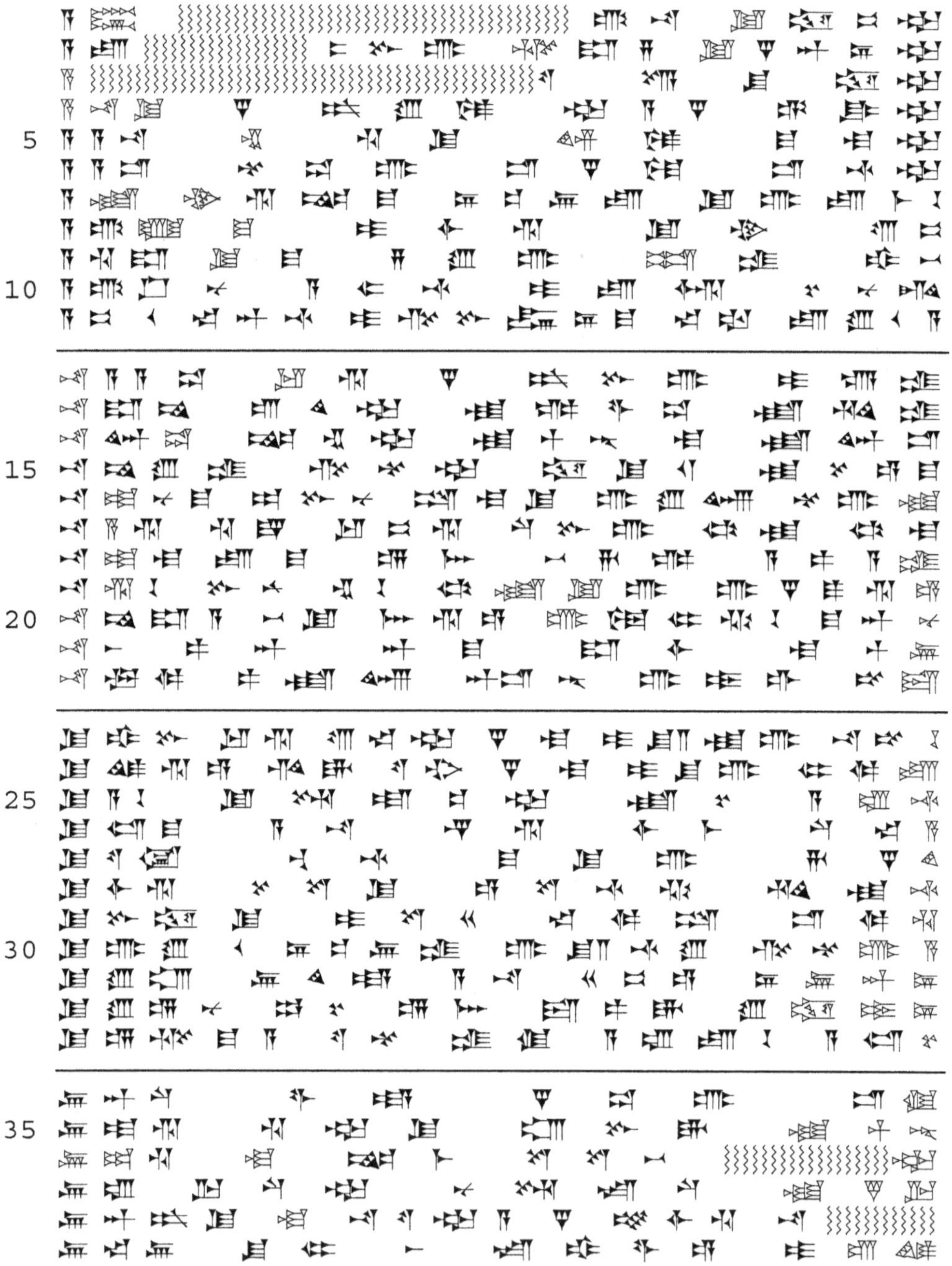

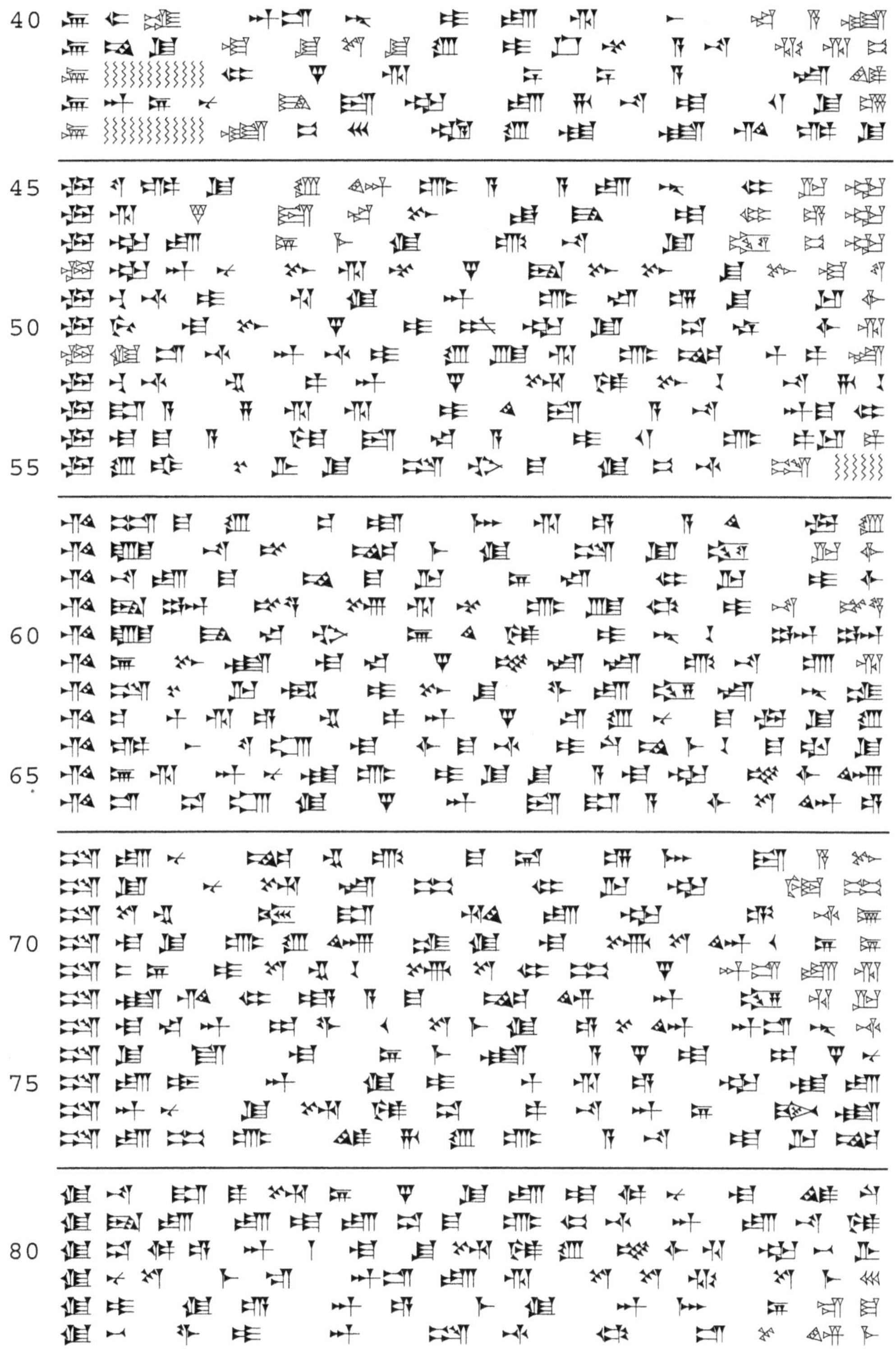

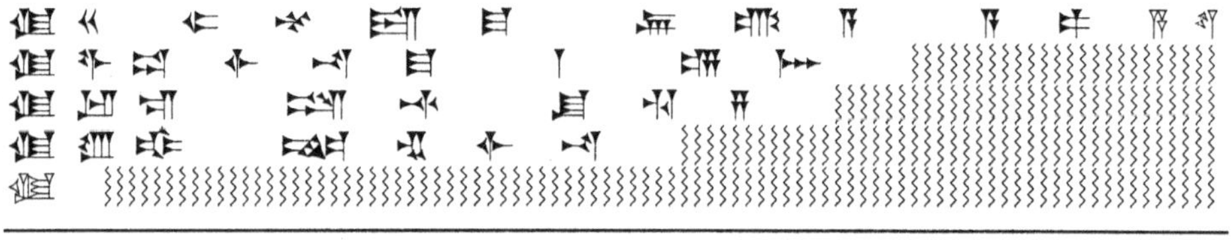

lines 89-119 missing

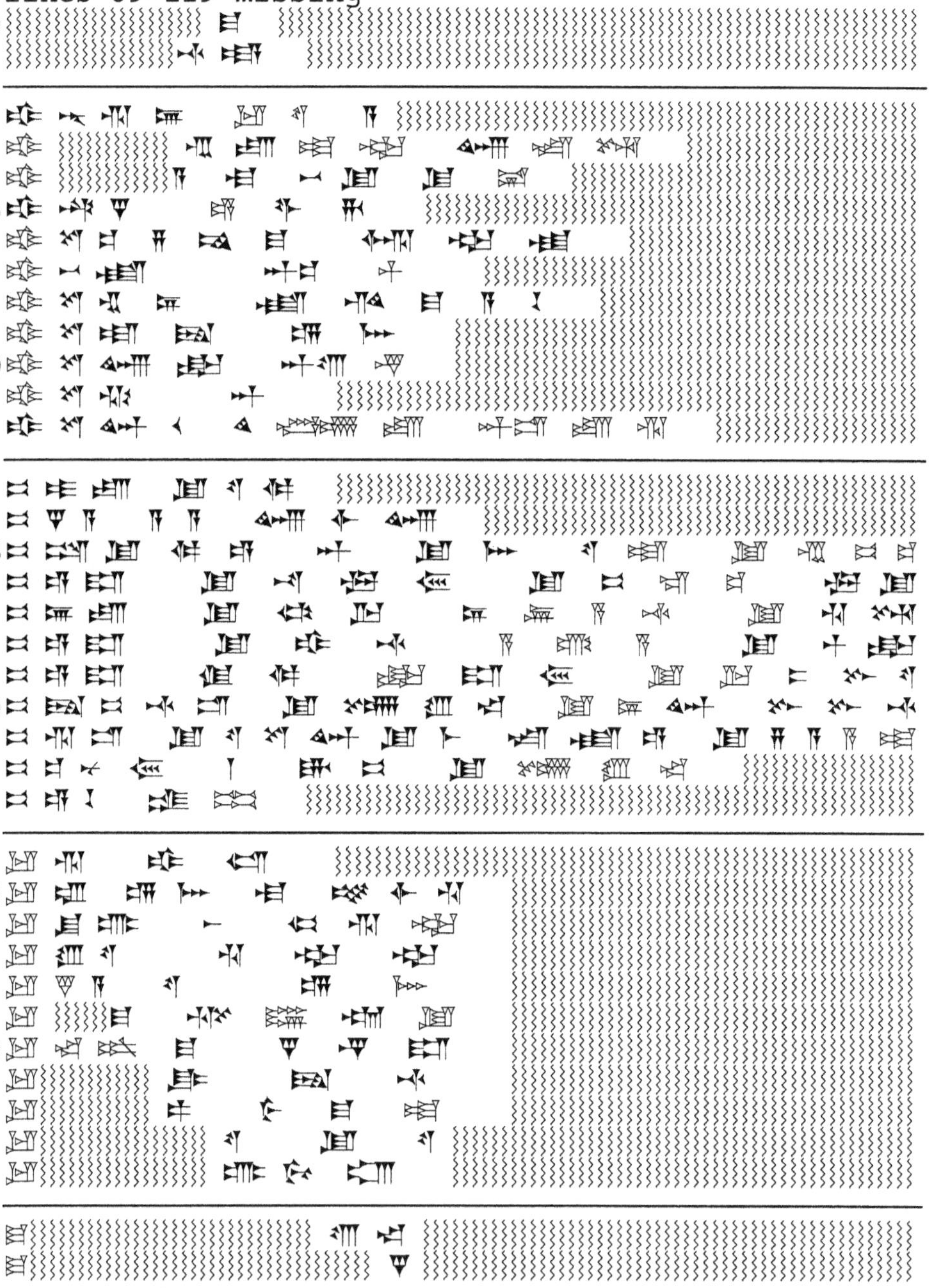

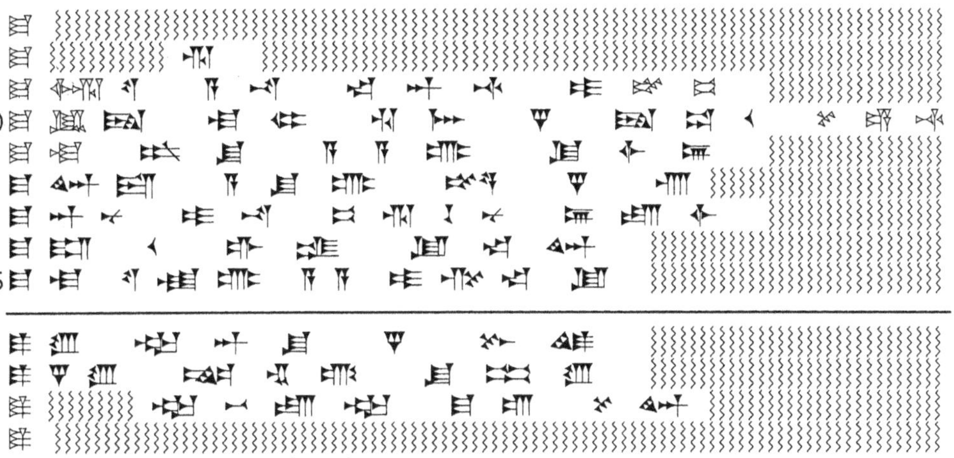

lines 170-175 missing

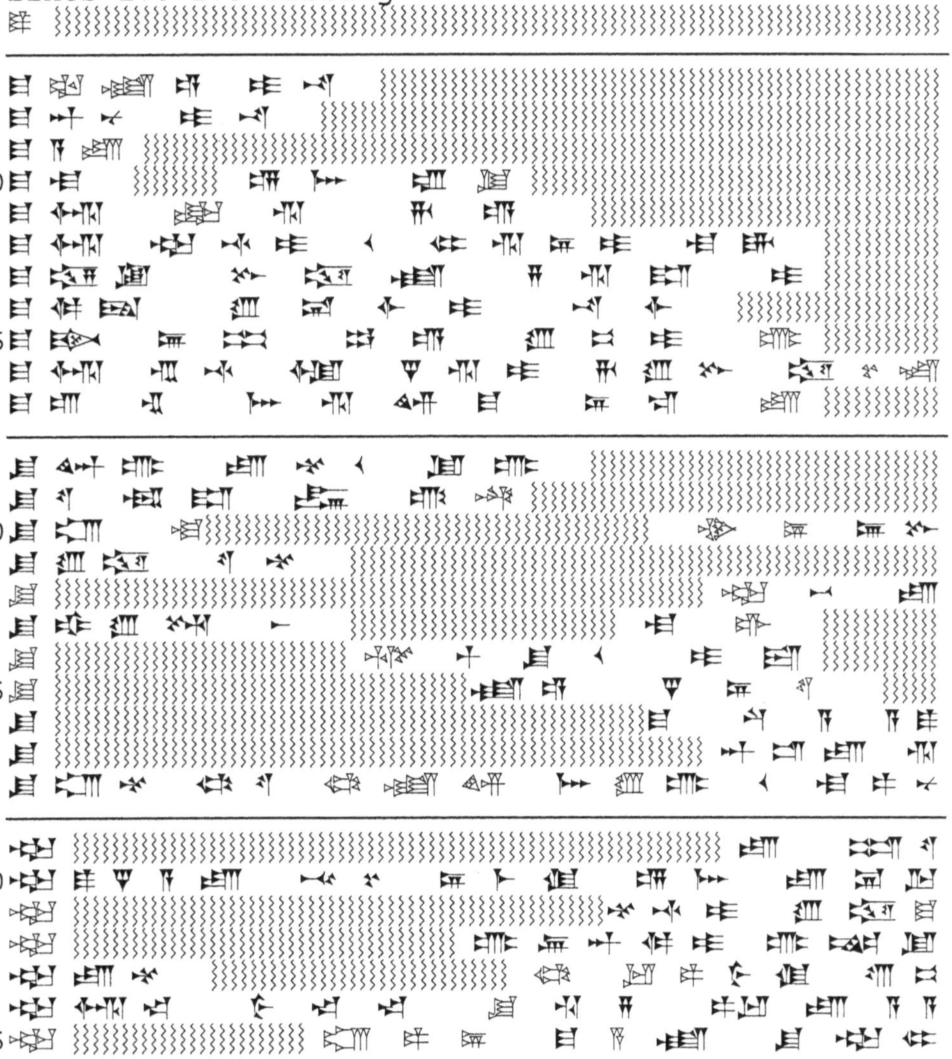

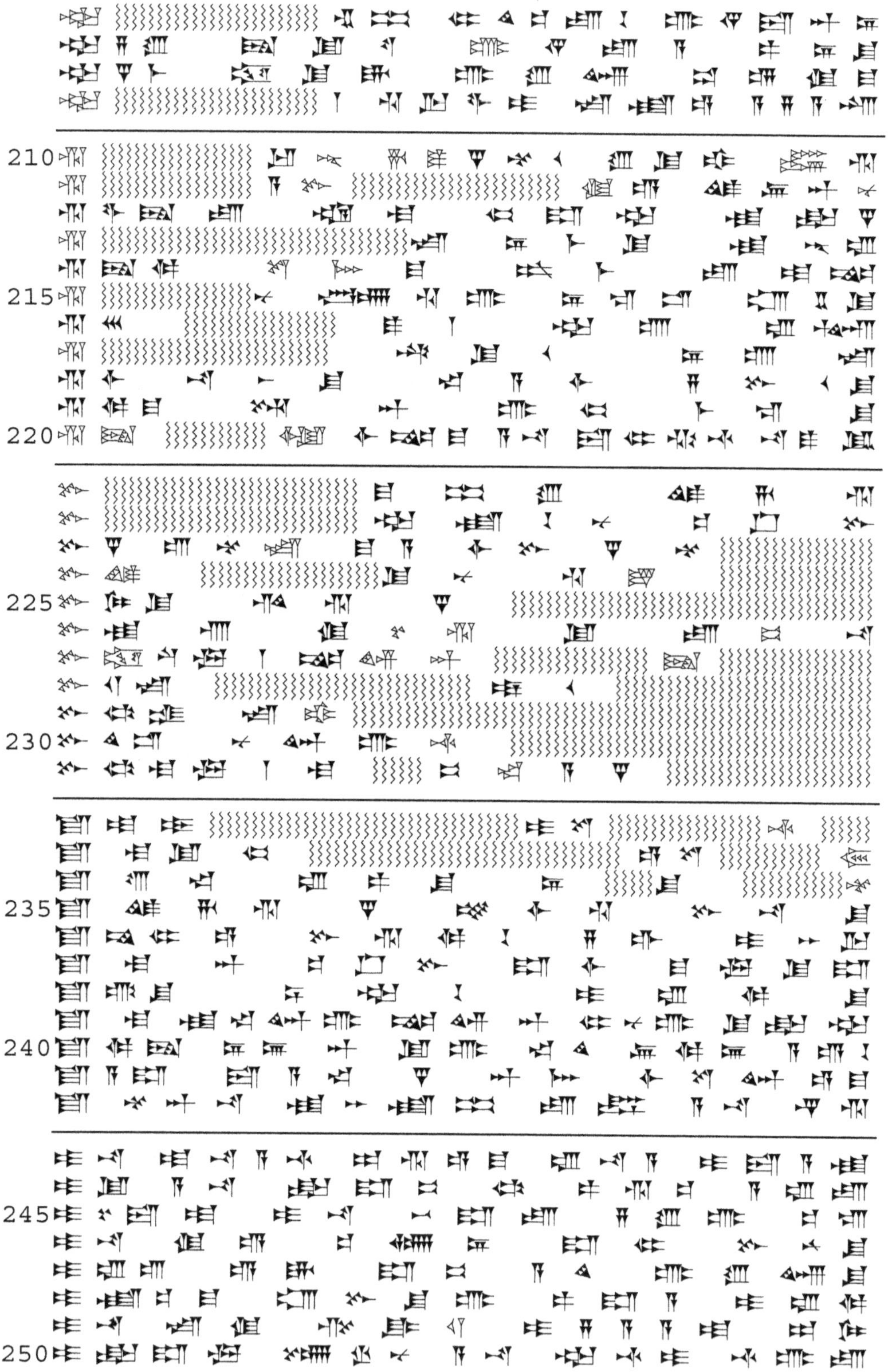

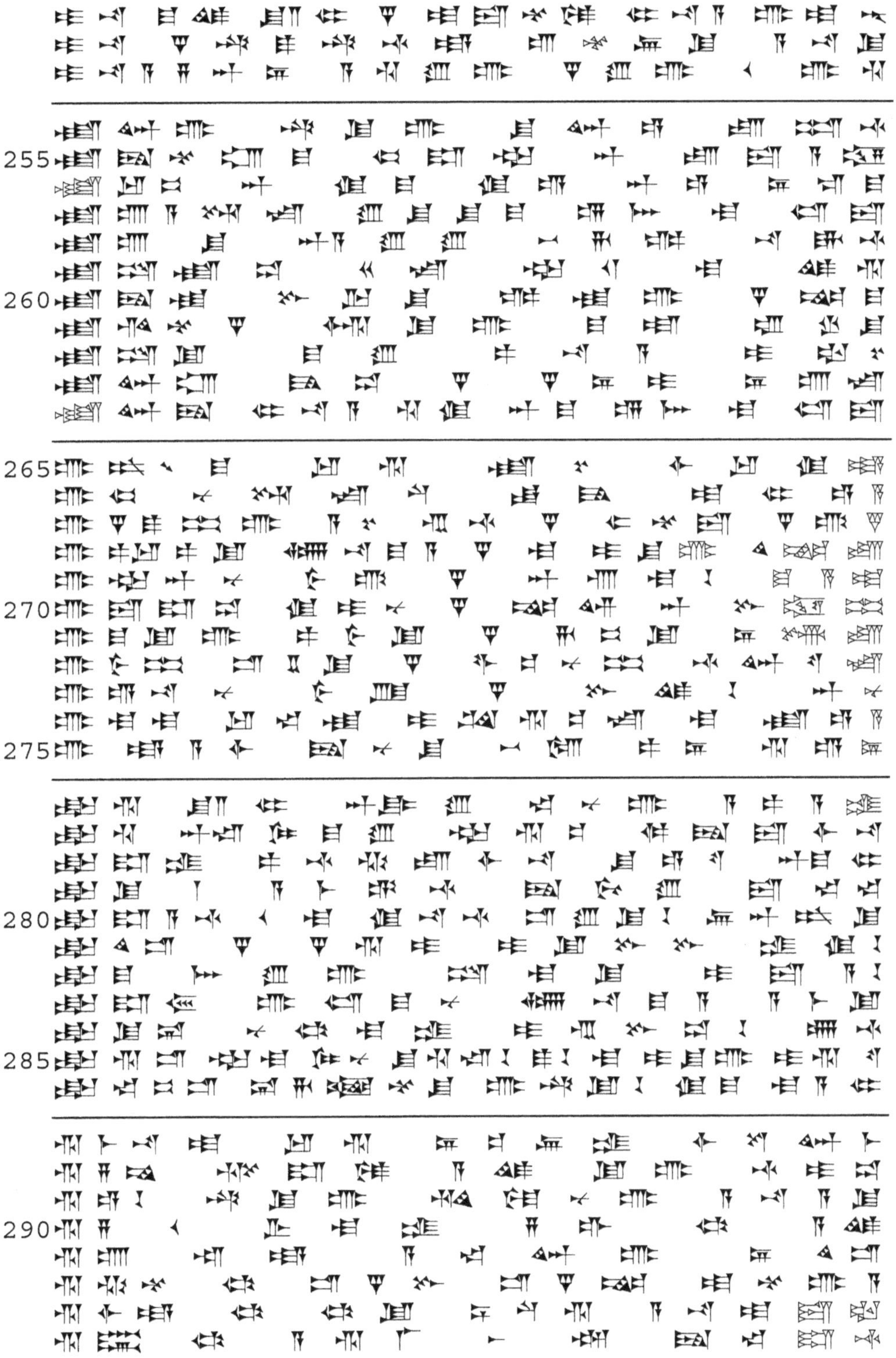

295

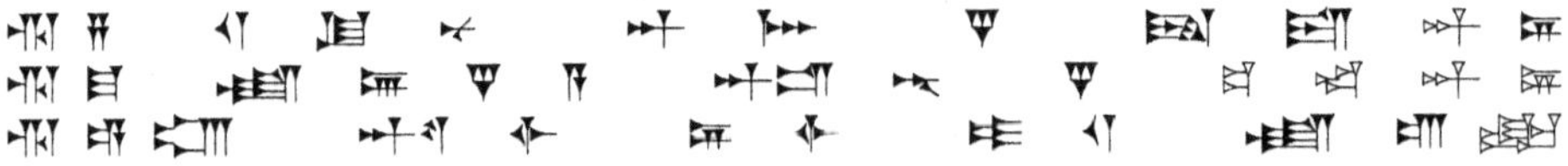

TRANSLITERATION

Strophe I – *Sufferer*

1 *a-š[i]š […] ga-na [lu]-uq-bi-ka*
2 *a-ta-×-[×-(×)] tap-pu-ú [n]am-ra-ṣa*$^?$ *[l]u-šá-an-ni-ka*
3 *[a- …]-×-tú kar-šu-uk-ka*
4 *[a-na-ku*$^?$*] šá šum-ru-ṣu ka-a-šá lud-lul-ka*
5 *a-a-na* [E]N *pak-ku [i]m-ṣu ma-la-ka*
6 *a-a-iš mu-du-ú iš-šá-nin iš-ti-ka*
7 *a-[li m]un-dal-kúm-ma ni-is-⌜sa⌝-ta lu-ú-ta-me-šú*
8 *a-ga-m[ir-m]a i-ši-ri lu-mun* ŠÀ-*bi*
9 *a-ḫu-ra-[k]u-ma za-ru-ú š[i]m-tum ub-til*
10 *a-ga-rin-nu a-lit-ti i-ta-ar* KUR NU GI$_4$
11 *a-bi u ba-an-ti i-zi-bu-in-ni-ma ba-al ta-ru-u-a*

Strophe II – *Friend*

12 *[n]a-a-a-du ⌜ib⌝-ri šá taq-bu-ú i-dir-tum*
13 *[n]a-ra-am saḫ-ḫi-ka tu-šak-pi-du le-mut-tum*
14 *[n]a-aʾ-[d]u ṭè-en-ka tu-maš-šil la le-ʾ-iš*
15 *na-am-ru-tum zi-mu-ka uk-ku-liš tu-še-e-ma*
16 *na-a[d]-nu-ma ab-bu-nu il-la-ku ú-ru-uḫ mu-ú-t[u]*
17 *na-⌜a⌝-ri ḫu-bur eb-bé-ri qa-bu-ú ul-tu ul-la*
18 *na-a[ṭ]-la-ta-ma* UN.MEŠ *mit-ḫa-riš a-pa-a-t[um]*
19 *na-⌜ṭal*$^?$*⌝-šú bu-kúr en-šú ul-⌜li⌝-[l]u-ú ú-šá-áš-re-[e]*
20 *n[a]-am-ra-a be-lu meš-re-e ⌜ú⌝-dam-mi-iq-šú ma-an-[nu]*
21 *n[a]-ṭil pa-an* DINGIR-*ma ra-ši la-mas-[sa]*
22 *n[a]-aq-di pa-li-iḫ* ^{d}*iš-tar ú-kám-mar ṭuḫ-[da]*

Strophe III – *Sufferer*

23 *ku-up-pu ib-ri* ŠÀ-*ba-ka šá la i-qát-tu-ú na-gab-[šú]*
24 *ku-mur-re-e gi-piš tam-tim šá la i-šu-ú mi-ṭi-[ta]*
25 *ku-a-šú lu-uṣ-ṣi-iṣ-ka li-mad a-l[ak-ti]*
26 *qú-lam-ma a-na sur-ri ši-me qa-ba-⌜a⌝-[a]*
27 *ku-ut-tùm gat-ti ma-ku-ú ḫa-šá-ḫ[i]*
28 *ku-ši-ri še-te-ku e-te-ti-iq mut-tu-t[i]*
29 *ku-bu-uk-ku i-te-niš ba-ṭi-il iš-di-[ḫu]*
30 *ku-ú-ru u ni-is-sa-tum ú-qát-ti-ru zi-mu-[ú-a]*
31 *ku-ru-um sa-ḫi-ia a-na neš-bé-e né-s[a-an-ni]*
32 *ku-ru-un-nu nap-šat* UN.MEŠ *ṭa-pa-piš ru-u[q-qan-ni]*
33 *ku-un-nam-ma-a u*$_4$*-mu dum-qí a-lak-ta-šú a-lam-[mad]*

Strophe IV – *Friend*

34 *sa-an-qa pi-ia šá-du-ú mil-[ki]*
35 *sa-ad-ri pak-ka-ku dub-bu-biš t[u-maš-šil]*
36 *[sa-a]p-ḫu [l]a*$^{?}$ *ṭè-me te-te-mid* × *[… -ka]*
37 *sa-miš ur-qa-ka nu-us-su-qa t[u-šá-lik]*
38 *sa-an-tak-ku [l]a na-par-ka-a šá taḫ-ši-ḫu na-*×*-[…*
39 *sa-ba-sa qad-mi ina su-up-pe-e i-s[aḫ*$^{?}$*-ḫur*$^{?}$*]*
40 *sa-lit-[t]um* ^{d}*iš-tar i-ta-ri ina b[a-a-li]*
41 *sa-am-ku* ⸢*la šu-te-šu*⸣*-ru i-rem-mu a-na i[k*$^{?}$*-ri*$^{?}$*-bi*$^{?}$*]*
42 *[sa-* ××*] mé-šá-ri qaq-dà-a su-ḫu[r]*
43 *sa-an-ni-nu [qa]r-da-ka ta-ḫa-na-at liš-ku-u[n]*
44 *[sa- … l]i-bé-eš nak-ru-ṭú li-gi-[sak-ku]*

Strophe V – *Sufferer*

45 *ak-tam-sak-ku [ru-*ʾ*u]-ú-a a-ta-ḫaz mi-[lik-ka]*
46 *aq-ri [šá da-b]a-bu sè-qar at-[mé-e-ka]*
47 *ak-ka-ta [né*$^{?}$*-m]e*$^{?}$*-qí*$^{?}$ *ga-na lu-u[q-bi-ka]*
48 *[ak]-ka-an-nu sér-re-mu šá iṭ-pu-pu šu-b[u-ul-tú]*
49 *ak-kat-ti-i pak-ki* DINGIR *ú-zu-un-šu ib-š[i]*
50 *ag-gu la-bu šá i-tak-ka-lu du-muq ši-r[i]*
51 *[ak-k]i-mil-ti* DINGIR*-ti-i šup-ṭu-ri ú-bil maṣ-ḫat-s[u]*
52 *ak-kat-ti* EN *pa-an šá uṣ-ṣu-bu-šú na-ḫa-šú*
53 *aq-ra-a ṣa-ri-ri i-ḫi-ṭa a-na* ^{d}*ma-mi*
54 *ak-la-ma-a nin-[d]a-ba-a i-liš ú-sap-p[a]*
55 *ak-ru-ub sat-tuk-ku il-tim-ma qí-bi-ti i[l*$^{?}$*- …*

Strophe VI – *Friend*

56 *gi-šim-ma-ru iṣ-ṣi meš-re-e a-ḫi aq-r[u]*
57 *gi-mir na-gab ne-me-qí il-lu-uk u[r-ši]*
58 *gi-na-ta-ma am-ma-tíš né-ṣú mi-lik i-lim*
59 *gi-it-mul* EDIN *[sé]r-re-mu ú-ṭu-ul i-n[a* EDIN*]*
60 *gi-mir qar-ba-tim ir-ḫi-ṣu i-ḫaš-šú mul-mul*
61 *ge-er bu-li la-ba šá taḫ-su-su ga-na bit-r[i]*
62 *gi-il-lat* UR.MAḪ *i-pu-šu pe-ta-as-su ḫaš-tum*
63 *gi-is maš-re-e* EN *pa-an šá qur-ru-nu ma-ak-ku-ru*
64 *gi-riš ina u*$_{4}$*-um la ši-ma-ti i-qa-am-me-šú ma-al-ku*
65 *ge-er-ri an-nu-tu-ú i-ku-šu a-la-ka taḫ-ši-iḫ*
66 *gi-mil du-um-qí šá* DINGIR *da-ra-a ši-te-*ʾ*e-e*

Strophe VII – *Sufferer*

67 *il-ta-nu ṭè-en-ga ma-nit* UN.MEŠ *ṭa-*⸢*a*⸣*-[bu]*
68 *il-lu nu-us-su-qu mi-lik-ka d[am-qu]*
69 *il-te-en zik-ra mut-ta-ka lut-t[i-ir]*

70 *il-la-ku ú-ru-uḫ dum-qí la muš-te-ʾu-u ì-l*[*í*]
71 *il-tap-ni i-te-en-šú muš-te-mi-qu šá* ⸢^{d}⸣[*iš-ta-ri*]
72 *il-li-gi-mi-ia-a-ma ṭè-em* DINGIR *as-ḫ*[*u-ur*]
73 *il-la-ba-an ap-pi u te-mi-qí e-še-ʾe* ^{d}*iš-tar-t*[*i*]
74 *il-ku ša la né-me-li a-šá-aṭ ab-šá-nu*
75 *il-ta-kan* DINGIR *ki-i maš-re-e ka-tu-ta*
76 *il-an-nu ku-uṣ-ṣu-du pa-na-an-ni lil-li*
77 *il-ta-qu-ú ḫar-ḫa-ru-ú a-na at-taš-pil*

Strophe VIII – *Friend*

78 *ki-na ra-áš uz-ni šá tuš-ta-ad-di-nu la mur-qa*
79 *ki-it-ta ta-at-ta-du-ma ú-ṣur-ti* DINGIR *ta-na-ṣu*
80 *ki-du-de-e* DINGIR *ana la šu-uṣ-ṣu-ru taḫ-ši-ḫu ka-bat-tuk*
81 *ki-nu-te me-si* ^{d}*iš-ta-ri te-te-eq te-me-*[*eš*]
82 *ki-i qé-reb* AN-*e šib-qí* DINGIR.MEŠ *né-s*[*i-ma*]
83 *qí-bít pi-i* DINGIR *il-ti ul iš-š*[*e-em-me*]
84 *ki-niš lit-mu-da-ma sa-ga-a a-pa-*⸢*a*⸣-[*tú*]
85 *ki-pi-du-ši-na-ma ana* UN.MEŠ × […
86 *ki-ib-si il-ti šu-ḫu-za* × […
87 *qé-ru-ub ṭè-en-ši-na* […
88 *k*[*i*-×] × [×] × […

Strophes IX–XI are missing.

Lines 89–119 are missing
It is very likely that lines 37–40b of the *Theodicy Commentary* are commentaries on the words belonging to lines 110–121 of the main text. Note especially line 37 of the *Theodicy Commentary* wherein all the terms begin with the syllable *AM*: …] ×-*RA*: *a-mur* ('I saw'): *am-mat*: *am-m*[*a-t*]*ú*$^{?}$ ('forearm' or 'strong'): *am-ma-raq* ('I am being scraped, rubbed away'): *ana za-ra-qú* ('to sprinkle, strew'): *am*-×-[: …

Strophe XI – *Sufferer*

120 …] *MA* × […
121 …]-×-*ti-ia* […

Strophe XII – *Friend*

122 *up-tar-ri-ir* ⸢*ip-laḫ*⸣ *a*-×-[…
123 [*UB-* …] *kab-ta-a*[*t*$^{?}$]-⸢*ka*⸣ *aḫ-*[*su*$^{?}$*-us*$^{?}$ …
124 [*UB-* …]-*a la be-lu KU U*[*Š* …
125 *ub-bal šá* ⸢*e*⸣-*pe-ḫa* […
126 [*u*]*p-te-eṣ-ṣa-am-ma ar-ka-tu* ×-[…
127 [*u*]*b-tel-li* ^{d}GIŠ.[BAR …
128 [*u*]*b-te-en-ni li-gi-ma-a-šú* […

129 [*u*]*p-te-ṣi-id* UN.MEŠ […
130 [*u*]*b-te-eḫ-ḫir* ^{d}*šà-s*[*ur* …
131 [*u*]*p-te-eq* DINGIR […
132 *ub-te-ʾ-u ḫi-ši*[*ḫ-ta iš-ta-ri*$^{?}$ …

Strophe XIII – *Sufferer*

133 *bi-i-ta lu-ud-di* × […
134 *bi-šá-a a-a aḫ-ši-iḫ* × […
135 *pí-il-lu-de-e* DINGIR *lu-meš par-ṣ*[*i lu-ka*]*b-*⸢*bi*⸣*-i*[*s*]
136 *bé-e-ra lu-na-ak-kis lu-kás*$^{!}$-⸢*si*$^{!}$*-is*$^{!}$⸣ *ak-lu*
137 *bi-ir-ta lu-ul-lik né-*⸢*sa-a-ti lu*⸣*-ḫu-uz*
138 *bé-e-ra lu-up-ti* ⸢*a*⸣*-g*[*a-a*] *lu-maš-šèr*
139 *bé-e-ra ki-di* <*šar*>*-ra-qiš* [*lu-u*]*r-tap-pu-ud*
140 *bi-it-bi-ti-iš lu-ter-ru-ba* ⸢*lu-ni*⸣*-ʾi bu-bu-ti*
141 *bi-ri-iš lu-ut-te-eʾ-lu-me su-le-e lu-ṣa-a-*[*a-ad*]
142 *pí-is-nu-qiš ana qer-bi lu-t*[*er*$^{?}$*-ru-ba* …
143 *bé-e-šú dum-*⸢*qu*⸣ ×× […

Strophe XIV – *Friend*

144 [*i*]*b-ri ub-lam* […
145 [*i*]*p-šet* UN.MEŠ *la taḫ-ši-ḫu* […
146 [*i*]*b-šu-ú ina ṣur-ri-*[*ka* …
147 [*ip*]*-ru-ud pak-ka-ka* […
148 [*ep-š*]*á-a-tú* UN.[MEŠ …
149 [*IB*-×]*-ma* NAM.<LÚ$^{?}$>.U$_{18}$.[LU …
150 [*ib-ba-t*]*aq-ma šá-sur-ra* […
151 [*IB* …] *LUL it-ti* […
152 [*IB* …] *PA šal-ma-a*[*t*$^{?}$ …
153 [*IB* …] × *TÚ lu-ut-*[…
154 [*IB* …] × *Ú GU UM* […

Strophe XV – *Sufferer*

155 [*MA* …] ŠÀ*-ba* […
156 [*MA* …] × *šá* […
157 [*MA* …] × […
158 ⸢*ma*⸣-[…] *RI* × […
159 ⸢*ma*⸣-[*ar*]*-tú a-na ba-an-ti i-*⸢*qab*⸣*-b*[*i* …
160 ⸢*ma*⸣-[*q*]*i-it la-mi* MUŠEN.MEŠ *šá id-du-u* [*še*$^{?}$*-e*$^{?}$*-ti*$^{?}$]
161 ⸢*ma*⸣-[*la*] *šum-šu a-a-ú ku-ši-ir* […
162 *ma-aʾ-da a-šu-ú* EDIN *šá ṣil-*× […
163 *ma-an-nu i-na bi-ri-šú-nu ir-ta-ši* […
164 *ma-ra u mar-tum lu-ba-ʾi* […
165 *ma-la ut-tu-ú a-a i-zi-ba lu* × […

Strophe XVI – *Friend*

166 *áš-ru ka-an-šu šá pu-ḫur* […
167 *áš-šá-ru ṭè-en-ga šu-qu-ru* × […
168 [*ÁŠ* ×] × *ka-bat-ta-ka ma-qit še-*ʾ-[…
169 [*ÁŠ* …] traces

170–175 missing

176 [*ÁŠ* …] traces

Strophe XVII – *Sufferer*

177 *ma-a*[*l*(-)*l*]*e-e i-na* × […
178 *ma-an-nu i-na* […
179 *ma-a-t*[*a* …] × […
180 *ma-la* × [×] × UN.MEŠ *šit-k*[*u-* …
181 *ma-ar š*[*a*]*r-ri ḫa-líp* […
182 *ma-ar ka-ti-i u mi-ri-ni-i la-biš* × […
183 *ma-aṣ-ṣar bu-uq-li ṣa-ri-ra i-*× [×]
184 *ma-di-id ru-uš-ši-i na-ši* × […
185 *ma-lil er-qu nap-tan ru-bi-i* ⸢*ú*⸣-[…
186 *ma-ar kab-ti ù šá-ri-i ḫa-ru-bu uk-*[*lat-su*]
187 *ma-qit* EN *meš-re-em-ma né-si t*[*a-* …

Strophe XVIII – *Friend*

188 *šu-*ʾ*u-ú ta-mu-u lu-ú* […
189 *šu-ut maḫ-ra in qá-ba*[*l* …
190 *šu-um l*[*a* … *mun*$^{?}$*-n*]*é-er-bu*
191 *šu-ru-uk* u_4*-mu* […
192 [*šu-* … *k*]*a*$^{?}$*-bat-ta*
193 *šu-up-ru-us ina* × […] × *LA* ⸢*MAR*⸣ × [××]
194 *š*[*u-* … *na*]*m-maš-šu-u i-da-*[××]
195 *š*[*u-* …] ×*-le-e šá-ni-t*[*ú*] ×[×]
196 *šu-*[…] ×*-ma qa-a-a-áš*
197 *šu-*[…] ^{d}*iš-ta-ri*
198 *šu-um-mu ul-tú u*[*l-li*$^{?}$]*-im*$^{?}$ *meš-r*[*u*]*-ú u la-pa-nu*

Strophe XIX – *Sufferer*

199 *ka-*[…] *ta-šim-tú*
200 *ka-áš-šá-a-ta kul-lat né-me-qí* UN.MEŠ *ta-mal-lik*
201 *k*[*a-* …]*-mu-ti-i ru-uq-m*[*a*]
202 [*ka-* …] *ú-sa-an-di-i ú-bil-lu*
203 *ka-ta-mu* [… *ul*$^{?}$ *ip*$^{?}$*-p*]*a-rak-ki* ŠÀ*-bi*
204 *ka-ar-ba šal-ba-ba* [*š*]*u-ḫu-za šap-ta-a-a*
205 [*ka-* … *ṭu*]*p-p*[*a-ni*] *ma-*⸢*a*⸣*-li šu-ka-mi*

206 [*ka-* …] *en-qu mi-ḫi-iṣ-ta-šú ú-paṭ-ṭa-an-ni*
207 *ka-ṣa-ru ed-lu-tú* ⌜*ú*⌝*-pat-ta-a pa-ni-šu*
208 *ka-šá-me uk-ku-piš ú-ru-uḫ du-un-qí-ma*
209 [*ka-* …] × *ana ḫu-ur-pi-i su-le-e a-ṣa-a-ád*

Strophe XX – *Friend*

210 [*RI* …] × *ip-si*[*l*] ⌜*ḫa-áš*⌝*-šá-mu-u ru-ku-ub* LUGA[L]*-ri*
211 [*RI* …] *a-b*[*u-* … *q*]*é-reb ḫur-sa-an-*[*nu*]
212 *ri-pi-it-ta nak-la ṣur-ra-ka tu-šar-šá*
213 [*RI* …]*-su né-me-qú tu-ṭar-rid*
214 *ri-id-di* [*te-meš*]*-ma šum-me ta-aṭ-pil*
215 [*RI* …]*-nu šúḫ-ḫu-ú né-si-iš tup-šik-ku*
216 *re-eš* […]*-áš ana ka-bidi šit-kun*
217 [*ri-it-pu-uš* ŠÀ*-ba-šú*] *pa*[*l*]*-ku-u ni-bit-su*
218 *re-ši na-aš-šu ba-a-ši ṣa-bu-u-šu*
219 *ri-di-ma us* DINGIR.MEŠ *ú-ṣur me-si-šu*
220 [*ri-id* …] ⌜*ù*?⌝ *lem-ne-ma a-na da-mi-iq-ti na-áš-kin*

Strophe XXI – *Sufferer*

221 [*BU-* …] × *ma-qu-ru ḫar-ḫa-ri*
222 [*BU-* …] × *ka-li-šú-nu is-ḫap-pu*
223 *bu-šá kit-mu-s*[*u*] *ma-a ši-bu šá mu-*×-[××]
224 [*pu-ḫur* …] ×*-ku-nu ḫu-bu*[*r* ××]
225 [*p*]*u-lum-ku ge-ri šá* × […
226 [*p*]*u-tu* NUN *ki-k*[*ur-r*]*i*? *lu ta-*[*b*]*i-na*
227 [*pu-u*]*q-qa-ak ana ṭè-*[*em* DINGIR …] × *I*[*D-* …] ×
228 [*p*]*u-lis-su* […] *TUR U* × […] ×
229 *bu-ul-tum su-u*[*p-*…] × […]
230 *pu-ḫi-iš nu-*ʾ*-ú-t*[*i*?] ×× [×] ×× […] ×
231 *bu-ul-la-ak ana la* × [×] × *BI* [*B*]*A*? *A ŠÁ* […] ×

Strophe XXII – *Friend*

232 *ša-at GAN* […] *I TE* × […] ⌜*TI*?⌝ ××
233 *ša la-lu ZUR* […] ×× *E TE* [×× *ZI*]*G*/*KI*]*Š*
234 *ša* ŠÀ*-ba rit-pa-šu ni-*×*-šu* × [×(×)*-m*]*u*
235 *ša ḫar-ḫa-ri šá taḫ-ši-ḫu bu-na-šu*
236 *ša-am-mé-e pu-ri-di-šú za-mar i-ḫal-liq*
237 *ša la* DINGIR *is-ḫap-pu ra-ši ma-ak-ku-ra*
238 *ša-ga-šu kak-ka-šú i-red-di-šu*
239 *ša la tu-ba-*ʾ*u-ú ṭè-em* DINGIR *mi-nu-ú ku-šìr-ka*
240 *ša-di-id ni-ir* DINGIR *lu-ú ba-ḫi sa-di-ir a-kal-šú*
241 *ša-a-ra ṭa-a-ba šá* DINGIR.MEŠ *ši-te-*ʾ*e-e-ma*
242 *ša* MU.AN.NA *tu-ḫal-li-qu ta-rab a-na sur-ri*

Strophe XXIII – *Sufferer*

243 *i-na ad-na-a-ti ab-re-e-ma šit-na-a i-da-a-tu*
244 *i-lu a-na šar-ra-bi ul pa-ri-is a-lak-ta*
245 *i-šad-da-ad i-na miṭ-ra-ta za-ru-ú* ^{giš}MÁ
246 *i-na qé-reb* ^{giš}*dun-ni ra-mi bu-kúr-šu*
247 *i-lak-kid lab-biš ra-bi a-ḫi ú-ru-uḫ-šu*
248 *i-li-iṣ-ma dup-pu-šu-ú pa-ra-a i-red-di*
249 *i-na su-qí zi-lul-li*[*š*] *i-ṣa-a-a-ad ap-lum*
250 *i-šar-ra-ak ter-den-nu a-na ka-ti-i ti-ú-ta*
251 *i-na ma-ḫar qád-mi šá ad-da-mu-ṣu mi-na-a ú-at-tar*
252 *i-na šá-pal áš-pal-ti-ia kit-*[*m*]*u-sa-ku a-na-ku*
253 *i-na-a-ṣa-an-ni a-ḫu-ru-ú šá-ru-ú u šam-ḫu*

Strophe XXIV – *Friend*

254 *le-ʾu-ú pal-ku-ú šu-ʾe-e ta-šim-ti*
255 [*l*]*i-it-mu-um-ma ṣur-ra-ka* DINGIR *ta-da-a-aṣ*
256 [*l*]*i-ib-bi* DINGIR *ki-ma qé-reb* AN-*e né-si-ma*
257 *le-é-a-us-su šup-šu-qat-ma* UN.MEŠ *la lam-da*
258 *li-pit* ŠU ^{d}*a-ru-ru mit-ḫa-riš na-piš-ti*
259 *li-il-li-du mìn-su ka-liš la mur-ri*
260 *li-it-tu bu-ur-šu reš-tu-ú šá-pil-ma*
261 *li-gi-mu-šá ar-ku-ú ma-ṣi šit-tin-šu*
262 *li-il-lu ma-ru pa-na-a i-al-lad*
263 *le-ʾu-um qar-du šá šá-ni-i ni-bit-su*
264 [*l*]*i-ʾi-id mi-na-a pak-ki* DINGIR-*ma* UN.MEŠ *la lam-da*

Strophe XXV – *Sufferer*

265 *ú-taq-qam-ma ib-ri li-mad ši-ib-qí-i*[*a*]
266 *ú-ṣur nu-us-su-qa sè-qar at-mé-e-*⸢*a*⸣
267 *ú-šá-áš-qu-ú a-mat kab-tu šá lit-mu-da šá-ga-š*[*á*]
268 *ú-šap-pa-lu dun-na-ma-a šá la i-šu-*⸢*ú*⸣ *ḫi-bi*[*l-ta*]
269 *ú-ka-an-nu rag-ga šá an-zil-la-šú m*[*a-a-ad*]
270 *ú-ṭa-ra-du ki-i-nu šá ṭè-em* DINGIR *pu-u*[*q-qu*]
271 *ú-*⸢*ma*⸣*-lu-ú pa-šal-lu šá ḫa-bi-lu ni-*[*ṣir-ta*?]
272 *ú-raq-qu iš-pik-ku šá pi-is-nu-qu ti-ʾ-ut-*[*su*]
273 *ú-dan-na-nu šal-ṭu šá pu-ḫur-šú an-n*[*u*]
274 *ú-la-la ib-ba-tu i-dar-ri-is-su la le-e-*[*a*]
275 *ú ia-a-ši et-nu-šu* EN *pa-ni re-dan-n*[*i*]

Strophe XXVI – *Friend*

276 *šar-ri qád-mi* ^{d}*nar-ru ba-nu-ú a-pa-a-t*[*um*]
277 *šar-ḫu* ^{d}*zu-lum-ma-ru ka-ri-iṣ ṭi-iṭ-ṭa-ši-na*
278 *šar-ra-tum pa-ti-iq-ta-ši-na šu-e-tú* ^{d}*ma-mi*
279 *šar-ku ana a-me-lut-ti et-gu-ru da-ba-ba*

280 *sar-ra-a-tú u la ki-na-tu iš-ru-ku-šú sa-an-tak-ku*
281 *šar-ḫi-iš šá šá-ri-i i-dab-bu-bu dum-qí-šú*
282 *šar-mi meš-ru-ú il-la-ku i-da-a-šú*
283 *šar-ra-qiš ú-lam-ma-nu dun-na-ma-a a-me-lu*
284 *šar-ku-uš nu-ul-la-tum i-kap-pu-du-šú ner-ti*
285 *sar-ri-iš ka-la lum-nu šu-ḫu-zu-šú áš-šú la i-šu-ú i-ri-tú*
286 *šar-ba-bi-iš uš-ḫa-ram-mu-šu ú-bal-lu-šú ki-ma la-a-mi*

Strophe XXVII – *Sufferer*

287 *re-me-na-at ib-ri ni-is-sa-tum ši-te-ʾe-me*
288 *ri-ṣa-am nam-ra-ṣu a-mur lu-ú ti-i-du*
289 *re-e-šú pal-ku-ú mut-nen-nu-ú a-na-a-ku*
290 *ri-ṣa u tuk-la-tum za-mar ul a-mur*
291 *re-bit* URU-*ia a-ba-ʾu-ú né-ḫi-iš*
292 *ri-ig-mu ul iš-šá-pu iš-šá-pil at-mu-ú-a*
293 *re-ši-ia ul ul-lu qaq-qa-ri a-na-aṭ-ṭ*[*a-al*]
294 *re-šiš ul a-dal-lal ina* UKKIN *it-ba-*[*ra-ti*]
295 *ri-ṣa liš-ku-nu* DINGIR.MEŠ *šá id-da-*[*an*]*-ni*
296 *re-ma li-ir-šá-a* ^{d}*iš-tar šá i*[*z-ba-an-ni*]
297 *re-e-um* ^{d}UTU-*ši ni-ši i-liš li-saḫ-ḫ*[*ir*]

TRANSLATION

Strophe I – *Sufferer*

1 Wise one, [...] come, [let] me tell you,
2 ...[.(.)] companion, [let] me recount to you [(my) pl]ight.
3 [...] .... [...] .. in your stomach (i.e. the seat of emotions),
4 let [me$^{?}$], who am greatly in distress, praise you always.
5 Where is the wise person who equals you?
6 What learned man can measure up you?
7 Where is the sage whom can I recount my grief?
8 I am finished (i.e.: exhausted). Anguish has come straight to me (i.e.: has attacked me).
9 I was the youngest child. Fate struck (my) begetter (i.e.: my father died);
10 the womb who bore me (i.e.: my real mother), headed for the Land-of-No-Return.
11 My father and my mother have left me (behind) with no guardian.

Strophe II – *Friend*

12 My attentive friend, what you have said is *dreadful* (lit.: misery).
13 Beloved one, (what) *is brewing in* your meadow (i.e.: your mind) is bad.
14 You have *reduced* (lit.: made equal to) your attentive intelligence into (that of) an incompetent (person),
15 you make your shining appearance (become) very dark.
16 Our fathers *have been given*, but *they shall* go the path of death (before us):
17 "I shall cross the river Hubur," (so) it has been said since ancient time.
18 When you look at people, the numerous (i.e.: mankind) as a whole,
19 does any son of a poor man become rich by *lo*[*oki*]*ng*$^{?}$ at him?
20 Who has made the *glorious* (lit.: shining) wealthy man *enjoy favour* (lit.: favourable)?
21 The one who serves (a) god has his protective-spirit,
22 the one who is in danger but reveres (a) goddess amasses wealth.

Strophe III – *Sufferer*

23 My friend, your heart is a water-source whose spring will never *dry up* (lit.: ends),
24 (the) *total mass* (lit.: surges) of the vast sea which *is undiminished* (lit.: has no decrease).
25 (But) I will question you; take note of my *p*[*oint*] (lit.: my course);
26 listen to me, for a moment, hear *what I am saying* (lit.: my saying).

27 My physique is overwhelmed, poverty is my needs;
28 I have missed my gain, my manliness is gone;
29 (my) strength is enfeebled, (my) income has run out;
30 depression and grief (have) blackened my appearance.
31 The *harvest* (lit.: food ration) of my meadow is far *below* (lit.: for) [my] satisfaction,
32 the *kurunnu*-beer, (the source of) people's life, is far from [my] contentment.
33 Can days of bliss be assured? I will understand the *point* (lit.: the way)!

Strophe IV – *Friend*

34 Verified are my words (lit.: mouth); [my] adv[ice] is (firm like) a mountain.
35 You [*turned* (lit.: made equal to)] your well-balanced thinking into an incoherent speech,
36 you *have made* (lit.: imposed) [*your* …] *shaken* and senseless,
37 you have made your well-chosen *thoughts* (lit.: green) suitable for a rogue.
38 Constant and never-ending is .. [..] which you desire.
39 In (response to) supplication, (the) furious pre-eminent being (i.e., divine being) will *t*[*urn* back$^{?}$];
40 (the) friendly goddess will return in (response to) be[seeching];
41 they (i.e., the gods) have mercy on the buried and misguided one in response to (their) *p*[*rayers*]/*o*[*ffering*].
42 Seek the ever-lasting [… of] justice.
43 your tenacious [*war*]*rior*$^{?}$ will establish help.
44 [M]ay […] go away and may ... grant you mercy.

Strophe V – *Sufferer*

45 I bow to you, my [frien]d, I have taken [your] ad[vice],
46 precious [*conversa*]*tion*, the words of [your] speech.
47 Come, let me [tell] you [(about) wis]dom:
48 Has the wild-ass, the onager, which was sated with e[ars of barley],
49 paid attention (lit.: has his ear) to the one who guarantees divine wisdom?
50 Has the savage lion who always ate the *best* meat,
51 (ever) brought *maḫṣatu*-flour-offering [in order to] appease [a furio]us godhead?
52 For the guarantor, did the rich man whose wealth is multiplied
53 examine valuable red-gold for Mami?
54 Have I held back cereal-offerings? I pray to (the) god;
55 I have (daily) prayed . […] with the regular offering to (the) goddess.

Strophe VI – *Friend*

56 Date palm, tree of wealth, my esteemed brother,
57 sum of all wisdom, jewel of s[agacity],

58 you are *right* (lit.: permanent), but, like the land, the counsel of (the) god *prevails* (prob. lit.: strong).
59 (But), i[n the steppe], look at the *perfect* (*animal*) of the steppe, the onager:
60 the arrow will *bring down* the one who trampled all the (cultivated) meadowland.
61 Come, *think about* (lit.: look carefully at) the lion, the attacker of livestock, which you mentioned (earlier),
62 (for) the crime which the lion committed, a pit opened up for it.
63 The one who is assigned wealth, the rich man who piled up treasures,
64 like the Fire-God, the ruler will burn (him) before his time (lit.: his destiny, i.e., predestined time for one's death).
65 Do you wish to go the way these (people/things) have gone?
66 Always seek the ever-lasting *blessing of favour* of the divine-beings.

Strophe VII – *Sufferer*

67 Your reason is (like) the north-wind, a pleasant breeze for the people,
68 chosen reasoning is your f[ine] counsel.
69 (But) let me reply (just) one word:
70 Those who do not seek (the) god (i.e., do not honour gods) go the way of *success*,
71 (while) someone who thinks of (the) goddess could become poor and impoverished.
72 In my youth, I searched for the reasoning of (the) god,
73 with the mark of respect and benedictions, I sought (the) goddess.
74 I bear a yoke as a corvée which (brought) no gain (v.: wisdom),
75 (but) (the) god has imposed (on me) poverty instead of riches.
76 A cripple went up above me; a fool moved forward away from me;
77 (while) rascals have moved up (in society), I have fallen (so) low (in society).

Strophe VIII – *Friend*

78 Righteous one, one who possesses wisdom (lit.: ear), what you *have* pondered is not rational.
79 Have you forsaken the truth? Do you despise the *order* (lit.: plan) of (the) god?
80 Do you not wish to be mindful of (lit.: make your heart to obey) the rituals of (the) god?
81 Do you bypass and neglect the correctness of the rites of (the) god and (the) goddess?
82 Like the centre of the heavens, the plan of (the) god are dis[tant],
83 the command of (a) god and (a) goddess is not hea[rd],
84 (but) human beings are *well* (lit.: rightly) acquainted with rituals.
85 Their (human) efforts, to the people [...
86 they were taught the path of (a) goddess . [...

87 Their (people's) reasoning is close […
88 . [.] . [.] . […

Strophes IX–XI are missing.

lines 89–119 are missing:

120 …] .. […
121 …] ... […

Strophe XII – *Friend*

122 He has been scattered and he has become afraid of .. […
123 […] your mind, I [*have*? *listened*? *to* …
124 […] . without the lord, .. […
125 I carry which/whom I block […
126 [He] has crushed the long . […
127 The Fire (or Fire-God) has destroyed […
128 (but) he (or I) looked after his/its bud (i.e., offspring …
129 He (or I) has shattered the people […
130 [I] was chosen by the Wo[mb (i.e., the Mother-Goddess) …
131 I have given heed to (the) god […
132 I have sought the things d[esired by (the) goddess? …

Strophe XIII – *Sufferer*

133 I will abandon the house . […
134 I will want no property . […
135 I will disregard the cultic duties of (the) god, [I will t]rample on the rites.
136 I will slaughter the chosen (sheep), I will consume the foods/bread(-offering).
137 I will walk a great distance, I will get (to) distant places.
138 I will open a barrier (of the canals) and send a flood.
139 Like a robber, I will roam over countryside.
140 From house to house, I will go (lit.: enter), I will drive away hunger;
141 I will roam around to the other side, I will prowl the streets.
142 Wretchedly, I will en[ter?] inside […
143 Distant, good-fortune, .. […

Strophe XIV – *Friend*

144 My friend, it (or I) brought […
145 The acts of people which you do not wish […
146 there are in [your] heart […
147 Your reasoning has been disturbed […
148 [the de]eds of people […

149 [..]., manki[nd? …
150 The womb [was cut o]ff and […
151–154: *too fragmentary to translate.*

Strophe XV – *Sufferer*

155–158: *too fragmentary to translate.*
159 A daughter will speak to (her) mother […
160 The bird-catcher who cast [the net] has fallen.
161 [Wh]at[ever] his name is, who […] profit […]
162 Many are living creatures of the steppe which .. […
163 Who among them has got […
164 I will seek a son or a daughter […
165 Whatever I find, will not leave, may . […

Strophe XVI – *Friend*

166 The humble and submissive one, who the assembly/all [of …
167 Your masterly reasoning, superb . […
168 [..] . your mind, fallen .. […
169 […] *traces only*

170–175 *missing*

176 […] *traces only*

Strophe XVII – *Sufferer*

177 .... in . […
178 Who in […
179 The lan[d …] . […
180 As much as . [.] . people .. […
181 The son of a king is clad with […
182 the son of a weak and naked man is clothed with . […
183 The guardian of malt, flashing gold .. [.]
184 the one who measures gold carries . […
185 the one who eats vegetables . […] the banquet of the prince,
186 (for) the son of an honourable and rich man, a carob-tree is [his] sustenance.
187 The rich has fallen, . […] is far away.

Strophe XVIII – *Friend*

188 Master, taking an oath shall be . […
189 Those who face in the mids[t of …
190 The name n[ot … fug]itive.
191 The day/fever is prolonged […
192 [… m]ind?.

193 He/it was excluded/cut off […] …. [..]
194 . [… an]imals, .. [..]
195 . […] ... something el[se] . [.]
196 . […] .. generous.
197 . […] goddess —
198 (that) is the law of rich and poor from an[cient ti]me (lit.: di[stant ti]mes).

Strophe XIX – *Sufferer*

199 . […] discernment,
200 you have gained all the wisdom, you have counselled people.
201 . […] ... is distant.
202 […] of fowler, carried.
203 Covered […] my heart [does not cea]se.
204 My lips are blessed, *articulate* (lit.: wise) and well taught,
205 [… ta]bl[ets] as well as the scribal art.
206 A wise […] whose *writing* makes me rejoice,
207 binding the locked-up people *brings him* (v.: me; them) *joy* (lit.: open his (v.: my; their) face).
208 The path of *blessing* (lit.: favour) might be *near* (lit.: soon),
209 […] . for an early harvest, I shall prowl around the streets.

Strophe XX – *Friend*

210 […] *turn[ed around*?], the crippled, the chariot of the king,
211 […] .. [… mi]dst of mountains.
212 You make your clever mind *go* (lit.: have) astray,
213 […] . wisdom you drove away,
214 [you (have) scorned] (divine) guidance and slandered (divine) laws.
215 […] . the brick hod is enlarged? (reaching) to a (great) distance,
216 The head/servant […] . to the mind, he/it was imposed.
217 [*His mind is very wide* (i.e., he is talented)] and *clever* (lit.: wide) is his *reputation* (lit.: name),
218 he is well honoured and has (all that) he wishes.
219 Follow the tradition of the god (v. gods), keep his cultic rites.
220 [*Leave* …] and the evildoers; be ready for well-being.

Strophe XXI – *Sufferer*

221 […] . the possessions of a rogue,
222 […] . all of them are villains.
223 The properties were gathered by saying: "the elder who .. [..].
224 [*gather* …] . of yours, a be[er-jar ..]."
225 [The b]oundary, the way of . […
226 [Infor]med prince, may the s[anctio]n be (my) shelter.
227 I am [pa]ying attention to the pl[an of (the) god …] .. […] .
228 Guide him [to] favour […

229 Shame, .. […] ... […] . […]
230 As a substitute, a mockery [.] .. […] .
231 I was cast to .. [.] ... [.] ... […] .

Strophe XXII – *Friend*

232 The one who/which . […] ... […] ...
233 the one who, wealth . […] .... [..] .
234 Of very wide heart (i.e., very wise) .... [.(.)].
235 As for the rogue whose prosperity you desired,
236 the *agility*[?] of his leg will soon be lost,
237 The villain who has no god may gain possession,
238 (but) a killer with his weapon pursues him.
239 If you do not seek the *will* of (the) god, what is your gain?
240 The one who bears the yoke of (the) god is indeed thin but his meal is regularly (*served*).
241 Seek constantly after the gratifying wind of (the) gods,
242 you shall regain at once what you have lost at the harvest time.

Strophe XXIII – *Sufferer*

243 I (have) looked into the world, but the *truth* (lit.: cases) is different,
244 the god does not block the path against the *šarrabu*-demon.
245 A father will pull a boat in a watercourse,
246 (while) his first-born is laid down on a *cot*.
247 (While) the big brother runs his way like a lion,
248 the younger son finds pleasure, (when) he drives a mule.
249 (While) the (first) son prowls around in the plaza like a vagrant,
250 the second (son) will give food to the needy.
251 What will I *gain* (lit.: increase) in front of the pre-eminent (i.e., the gods) before whom I have humbled myself?
252 I indeed keep bowing (even) at the *feet* (lit.: bottom) of the men of lower status than myself,
253 (and) a rich and prosperous junior person despises me.

Strophe XXIV – *Friend*

254 Competent and *wise* master of discernment,
255 (because) your heart is angered, you *turn to* (the) god with disrespect.
256 The divine (lit.: of (the) god) mind is as far as the centre of the heavens,
257 *comprehending it* (lit.: its competence) is very difficult; people cannot understand.
258 The creation of the hand of Aruru, altogether *living-creatures* (lit.: life),
259 why do the *human beings* (lit.: offspring), all of them, not *pay attention* (lit.: attentive)?
260 The first calf of a cow is inferior,

261 a later scion will *be* doubly *good as* (lit.: correspond to) it (i.e. the first calf).
262 The first son is born a fool,
263 (but) this second (son)'s reputation is capable and heroic.
264 Although one might be attentive, people cannot understand what the *divine* plan (lit.: plan of (the) god) (could) be.

Strophe XXV – *Sufferer*

265 *Pay heed* to me (lit.: wait attentively on me), my friend, learn my ideas,
266 examine the chosen word(s) of my speech:
267 They (people) extol the word of the important (man), who knows how to murder (people),
268 they also humiliate the *pitiable* (*man*) who *does* (v. has) no harm.
269 They take good care of the criminal whose abominations *are* m[any],
270 they send away the righteous one who pays attention to the wish of (the) god.
271 They fill the tr[easure] with the gold of a wrongdoer,
272 they empty the grain-bin, the fo[od] of a weak man,
273 they strengthen the man of authority, whose every (act) is cri[me].
274 They destroy the helpless and trample upon the powerless.
275 And as for me, the weak one, a rich man *keeps* persecuting me.

Strophe XXVI – *Friend*

276 The king of the pre-eminent (ones) (i.e., the gods) Narru (=Enlil), the creator the people,
277 the noble Zulummaru (=Ea), the one who pinched off their (people's) clay,
278 the queen, the one who shapes them (people), the mistress Mami,
279 gave *twisted* speech to humankind:
280 They (also) bestowed upon them (i.e., on mankind) lies and *falsehood* for all time.
281 (Therefore) they (i.e.: the people) proudly speak of the well-being of the rich:
282 "The king is the one at whose side wealth walks."
283 Men treat the *pitiable* (*man*) badly like a thief,
284 they *behave towards* him *maliciously*; they plan his murder.
285 Falsely all the bad things were taught to him (i.e., to the sufferer) because he has no guidance;
286 they will make him fall down like a powerless (man); they will extinguish him like glowing ashes.

Strophe XXVII – *Sufferer*

287 O my friend, you are very kind: Examine (my) grieving
288 help me, I have seen (lit.: saw) hardships, you shall know.
289 I am the *talented* one (lit.: whose head is wide), ever praying,

290 I found neither help nor aids at the moment.
291 I *tread* (lit.: go) the plaza of my city quietly,
292 (my) outcry (has) not become loud; my *voice* (has) been lowered.
293 I do not lift up my head high, I star[e] at the ground,
294 I do not praise the (assembly)-*mem*[*bers*] in the assembly like a slave.
295 May (the) gods who forsook me establish help (for me).
296 May (the) goddess who d[eserted me] have mercy on me.
297 May the shepherd (i.e., the human king), my Sun, gui[de back] the people to the god.

PHILOLOGICAL NOTES

Line 11 *a-bi u ba-an-ti*: While *abī*, literally 'my father,' is a normal term referring to one's own father, *bāntī*, literally 'my creatrix', is a poetic word indicating one's own mother. Probaly, the author chose the word *bāntī* instead of the more common term *ummī*, literally 'my mother', in order to create a rhyme with *abī*. Note also that *zārû*, literally 'seeding, begetter' and *agarinnu*, literally 'womb, brewer's mash', used in lines 9–10, are likewise poetic words referring to 'father' and 'mother' respectively.

ba-al ta-ru-u-a: The *tārû* is a derivative of (*w*)*arû*, 'to lead,' and indicates a foster-parent or guardian. Clearly the author used this word for a pun with KUR.NU.GI_4 (which can be read: *māt lā târi*), 'the Land of No-Return,' the last word of the previous sentence (line 10). Incidentally, *Theodicy Commentary* obv 5 equates *ta-ru-ú* with *ru-ub-bu*, i.e. 'to bring up.'[182]

In Strophe I, the sufferer complains that his parents had died when he was still young and left no caregiver. If he really was a royal counsellor or an apprentice as discussed in the introduction section above, it is hard to take this statement literally. It is difficult to believe that the sufferer had been an orphan without financial support, since the chances of success as a scribe or a scholar for an orphan without financial support would have been very low. With the sufferer's claim that he had no caregiver (line 11), he probably meant that he had not been raised by his own family but rather had been put out for adoption. We know of several cases in antiquity in which children adopted by scribes eventually became scribes themselves.[183]

Line 13: Literally, '(My) dear, what you made your meadows plan is evil.'

saḫ-ḫi-ka: This word is preserved on MSs B and G. This line is problematic mostly because *saḫḫu*, 'meadow,' does not yield good sense in the context. It is possible that this *saḫḫu*, 'meadow', somehow indicates 'mind, heart, sense,' because, in the *Babylonian Theodicy,* words related to 'spring,' e.g., *kuppu* (line 23); *nagbu* (line 23)[184] as well as 'green,' e.g., *urqu* (lines 37 and 57), are often used to indicate 'intelligence,' 'wisdom,' or 'good sense'.

Although Zimmern's emendation, *libbu-*(*bu*)*-ka*, 'your heart,'[185] yields better sense, it is hard to believe that two manuscripts could share the same mistake.

---

182 OSHIMA, forthcoming.

183 For an example, in the Neo-Babylonian period, of an adopted child receiving training to be a scribe from his adoptive father, see BEAULIEU 1992, pp. 103–105 and note 21. See also, WUNSCH 2003/4. p. 197; CHARPIN 2010, pp. 50–51.

184 For further discussion of *kuppu* and *nagbu* in the context of wisdom, see the commentary on line 23 below.

185 ZIMMERN 1895, p. 3. His reading was later followed by EBELING 1924, p. 6 and LANDSBERGER 1936, p. 44, but they read *lìb-bu*(?)*-ka*, clearly having noticed that the second sign cannot be in fact *BU*.

Lambert 1960, pp. 70–71 reads *saḫ-ḫi-ka* but translates "your *mind*". Von Soden 1990, p 147 basically followed Lambert's (or Zimmern's) rendering. Cf. also, Foster 2005, p. 915.

tu-šak-pi-du: It is true that *lemuttu kapādu* is normally taken to be an expression for 'to plan evil.' However, given the fact that the verb is in the subjunctive mode (which is confirmed by the *plene* writings on MSs B and G and by the parallelism with line 12), it seems that *saḫḫika* is the object of *kapādu* (Š-stem) while *lemuttu* is the predicate of a nominal sentence. My translation '(what) is *brewing*' is intended to convey the most common meaning of *kapādu*, 'to plan,' and the interpretation given in *Theodicy Commentary* obv 6: *tu-šak-pi-du* = *ka-pa-du* = *ṣa-ra-mu*, 'you make something/someone plan = to plan = to strive.'[186]

Line 16: It seems that the main message of this sentence is that fathers should die before their children. Note, e.g., von Soden 1990, p. 147: "Hingegeben waren unsere Väter, mussten (immer) den Weg des Todes gehen." Incidentally, Foster 2005, p. 915 offers a very different interpretation and translates this line: "Of course our fathers pay passage to go death's way." Judging from the context, however, Foster's interpretation seems less likely.

It is possible that this line is an allusion to an ancient popular saying. Note, for example, the funerary tablet of Yabâ, the queen of Tilgathpileser III (774–727 BCE) lines 3b–4 (Al-Rawi 2008, pp. 119–120):

3b ... *ina mu-te* NAM ZI-*ti*
4 *ik-šú-da-še-ma ur-ḫu* AD.MEŠ-*šú ta-lik*

3b ... *at the time of* (lit.: in) (her) death, the destiny of the *mortals* (lit.: life)
4 had captured her and she went the path of her fathers (i.e., ancestors).

Line 17: The institution of death as the inevitable fate is best recounted in the Old-Babylonian *Epic of Gilgamesh* from Sippar, col. iii 3–5 (George 2003, pp. 278–279):

3 *i-nu-ma* DINGIR.MEŠ *ib-nu-ú a-wi-lu-tam*
4 *mu-tam iš-ku-nu a-na a-wi-lu-tim*
5 *ba-la-ṭám i-na qá-ti-šu-nu iṣ-ṣa-ab-tu*

3 When the gods created mankind,
4 for mankind they established death,
5 (eternal) vigour, they kept for themselves.

The same notion is also found in an ancient didactic text, the *Nothing is of Value* (Níĝ-nam), 3–4 (Alster 2005, p. 273):

3 nam-úš-àm ⸢ḫa⸣-la lú-u$_{18}$-lu-kam
4 ⸢níĝ⸣-nam-a-ka-ni lú na-me ⸢la⸣-ba-an-ši-in-kar

3 Death is the share of man;
4 the consequences of his fate, no man can escape them.

Line 19 *na-⸢ṭal⸣-šú*: This line literally means: "Does (the action of) looking at him make any son of the poor rich?" Von Soden 1990, p. 147, note 19 a) reads the first word: *na-a*[*n*]-*šú*, and translates: "Erhoben war der Sproß eines Armen,

[186] Lambert 1960, p. 70.

irgendwer hatte [ihm] zu Reichtum verholfen." FOSTER 2005, p. 915 follows this interpretation. Yet, the traces attested in MS A suggest that the second sign is more like *LU*, *ṬU* or *RI* than *AN*. Thus I tentatively offer *na-*⌜*ṭal*⌝*-šú* as a possible reading of the first word of this line because of the rhyme with line 18, *na-a*[*t*]*-la-ta-ma*, and the contrast to line 21. If my restoration is correct, it seems that the author asserts that admiring rich people would make no-one rich and, instead of doing that, one should worship gods.

ul-⌜*li*⌝*-*[*l*]*u-ú*: Here I follow VON SODEN 1990, p. 147 19b) and take *ul-li-lu-ú* to be a by-form of *ullalla*.

Line 20 *n*[*a*]*-am-ra-a*: LAMBERT 1960, pp. 71 and 303 takes it to be a derivative of *marāʾu* and translates this word "fattened". Here, on the other hand, I take it to be an adjective, *namru* (*nawru*), 'shining, bright,'[187] and the long vowel *-ā* as the indication of the interrogative mode.

Line 23: Cleary the words *kuppu*, 'cistern,' and *nagbu*, 'deep-spring,' are used here as allusions to 'wisdom,' although it is not easy to see a semantic connection between wisdom and water-source. It is possible that the author of the *Babylonian Theodicy* used these words, *kuppu* and *nagbu*, to refer to the divine wisdom, particularly that of Ea, who was the god of wisdom and of water,[188] or of his son Marduk.[189] For example, CT 24, pl. 14, 48 (//KAV 51, rev 7) alludes to $^{d\,na\text{-}ag\text{-}bu\,(v\text{-}be)}$BAD among other names of Ea while ^{d}*lugal-a-ki-a* is explained to be ^{d}A-MAR.UTU *šá nag-bi*, 'Marduk of the deep-spring,' in the *Marduk Theology* (CT 24, pl. 50, BM 47406, line 2)[190].

Line 25 *a-l*[*ak-ti*]: The *Theodicy Commentary* line 8 equates *alaktu* to *ṭēmu*.[191] This equation *alaktu* = *ṭēmu* is already known in *Malku* = *Šarru* IV 114 among the words meaning either 'plan, design, oracle,' or 'wisdom, intelligence.'[192] My translation 'point' is to convey this interpretation given by the *Theodicy Commentary*. The same usage of this word is also attested in line 33 below. For the meaning of *alaktu*, see SCHWEMER 2010, p. 494, *contra* ABUSCH 1987, pp. 17 and 29.

Line 27 *ḫa-šá-ḫ*[*i*]: VON SODEN 1990, 148, note on line 27 reads *ḫa-a-t*[*i*], "hält mich darnieder." *CAD* M/1 follows von Soden's emendation, *ibid*., p. 140, *makû* A. However, my collation confirms that the second last sign is indeed *ŠÁ* as copied by Lambert in *BWL*.

---

187 Usually, however, with exception of slaves, *namru* is not used to describe a man but deities, see *CAD* N/1, pp. 239–244, esp. 244, 3 a).

188 For Enki/Ea being the god of water, see GALTER 1983, pp. 52–58; 80–84. For Enki/Ea being the god of wisdom, see *ibid*., pp. 95–103.

189 For Marduk being the god of water (and fertility), see OSHIMA 2006. For references to Marduk's wisdom in Akkadian prayers, see OSHIMA 2011, pp. 453–454.

190 For the edition, see PARPOLA 1995, pp. 398–401.

191 OSHIMA, forthcoming.

192 HRŮŠA 2010, pp. 98–101: *šibqu*, 'scheme', (111); *ûrtu*, 'plan', (112); *murqu*, 'intelligence', (113); *têrtu*, 'oracle', (115); *pakku*, 'wisdom', (118). These entries are followed by the words meaning 'counsel, consideration': *tašīmtu* = *milku* (119); *šitūltu* = *ditto* (120). Note also an unpublished OB lexical text which lists *ṭēmu*, *milku*, *šibqu*, and *tašīmtu* as Akkadian translations of the Sumerian word a-rá, *PSD* A/1, pp. 150–151.

Line 28 *še-te-ku*: The word is restored from the *Theodicy Commentary*. MS B has *ši-te-«ti»-ek*[193] while MS C has *ši-ti-QA*. The *Theodicy Commentary* explains *še-te-ku* to be *še-e-tú*: *e-te-qa*, 'miss, escape = pass by.'[194] Given this, I take the verb to be the stative of *šêtu* in G-stem, i.e., *šētēku*.

Although it seems be a scribal error, based the orthography on MS C, *ši-ti-qa*, one may suggest taking it to be the Gt-stem of a verb based on the root √*šʾq*, i.e., *šêqu* or *šiāqu*.[195] The exact meaning of this word still escapes us. If *ši-ti-QA* is not a scribal error for *ši-ti-ak* or the like, based on the *Theodicy Commentary*, one may suggest something like 'to disappear[?], pass[?], come to an end[?], abate[?]' as its possible meanings.[196] Given the context, one may speculate that it is the stative of *šēqu*/*šiāqu* Gt-stem, although *šitūq* is expected.

Incidentally, von Soden 1990, p. 148, note 28 a) speculates that *ši-ti-qa* in the *Babylonian Theodicy* is a scribal error for *ir-ti-qa*. However, because this word is preserved on MSs B, C and the ancient commentary, von Soden's suggestion for emendation cannot be supported.

Line 30 *ku-ú-ru u ni-is-sa-tum*: These words *kūru*, 'depression,' and *nissatu*, 'grief, wailing,' often allude to the symptoms of illnesses and to the pains caused by diseases. For example *Malqu* VII, 39–41:

39 *aṭ-ru-ud a-sak-ku aḫ-ḫa-zu šu-ru-up-pu-u ša* SU-*ka*
40 *ú-šat-bi qu-lu ku-ru ni-is-sa-tú šá pag-ri-ka*
41 *ú-pa-áš-ši-iḫ šer-a-ni mi-na-ti-ka* NU DÙG.GA.MEŠ

39 I drove away the *Asakku*-demon, *Aḫḫazu*-demon, the *shivering* (lit.: frost) from your body,
40 I removed the silence (e.g., despair), depression, and wailing from your flesh,
41 I eased the tendons of your *limbs from* whatever is unpleasant.

On the motif, 'one's looks become black because of illness or depression,' see, for example, Oshima 2011, pp. 288–289, 26":

26" [G]IM *zi-i-bi aṣ-ṣa-lim* ⌜*a*⌝-[*na-ku*]
26" [L]ike a black cumin, I turned black [I (did)].

Line 34 *šá-du-ú*: Given the context, it is clear that *šadû*, literally 'mountain,' is used as a metaphor referring to either firmness[197] or correctness of the sufferer's argument. In ancient synonym lists, *šadû* is attested as a synonym of *kinnû*/*ginnû*,

---

[193] It is very likely that the scribe was confused by *e-te-ti-iq* following this word and erroneously inserted *TI* between *TE* and *IQ*.

[194] Oshima, forthcoming.

[195] For *šêqu* or *šiāqu*, see *AHw*, p. 1226. Note also, von Soden 1957, p. 318.

[196] It is also possible that the scribe of MS C took it to be √*štq*, a cognate of Aramaic or Hebrew word, meaning 'to be/become quiet'. Note also that *Theodicy Commentary* line 8 explains *qa-a-lu* (i.e., *qâlu*, 'to be/become quiet, pay attention to') in line 26 of the main text to be *ša-ta-qa*. Because it is cited as the synonym of *qâlu*, it is evident that *šatāqu* here does not mean 'to split', but 'to be/become queit', as in the North-/West-Semitic cognates.

Incidentally, *CAD* E cites this line from the *Babylonian Theodicy* on p. 395 under *etēqu* A, 6 *šūtuqu*. Apparently it takes it to be the Š-stem (or Št-stem) of *etēqu* and reads *ši-te-ti-iq* with a variant *ši-ti-qa*. Needless to mention, we normally expect *šūtuq* (for N/L.B. and jB) or *šētuq* (N.Ass.) for Š-stem stative of *etēqu*.

[197] Cf. Streck 1999, pp. 89–90.

another word for 'mountain.' Note *Malku* = *Šarru* II 33: *kinnû* = *šadû*;[198] *ibid*., VIII 22: *ginnû* = *šadû*;[199] and LTBA II, 2, 6: [*g*]*i-nu-u* = *šad-du-ú*. Note also *Ludlul Commentary* rev 16: *kin-nu-u* KUR-*ú* (*šadû*).[200] Needless to say, *kinnû*/*ginnû* sounds very similar to *kīnu*, 'right, true,' or *ginû*, 'regular, normal.' Given these ancient synonym lists and the *Ludlul Commentary*, one might ask whether the author of the *Babylonian Theodicy* might have used the word *šadû* as some sort of word-play between the words *kinnû*/*ginnû* (a synonym of *šadû*) and *kīnu*/*ginû*.

Line 37 *ur-qa-ka*: This word normally means 'green, yellow' in Akkadian. However, in the *Babylonian Theodicy*, it is used with the meaning 'good sense, wisdom', as it is clear from *Theodicy Commentary* obv 12: *ur-qa* = *ṭè-e-mu*, 'green = sense.'[201] Incidentally, *CAD* S, p. 193, *sasqû* d) suggests reading *tas-qa-ka*, 'your *sasqû*-offering.' However, given *la mur-qa* (v. *u*[*r*?-*qa*]) in line 78, this is unlikely.

Line 39 *qad-mi*: *Theodicy Commentary* obv 13–14: *qad-m*[*u*] = ⸢*re-e*⸣-[*ši*] = *ana qu-ud-mu* = *maḫ-ri*, 'preeminent = head, beginning, first = before, in presence of = front.'[202] Note also LTAB II, 1 vi 30 and *ibid*., 2 vi 366: *qu-úd-mu* = *re-e-ši* (v. *maḫ-ru*). Note also *Malku* = *Šarru* III 72: *qudmu* = *maḫru*.[203] The words *qudmu* and *qadmu* initially referred to a minor god (or gods) from the circle of Ištarān or Madānu who had a role as a divine judge.[204] However, it seems that, later, it lost this original meaning and was used as an epithet for a god in general as is clear from a god list, CT 25, 18, ii 9: *qa-ad-mu* = *i*-[*lu*]. For further discussion of the god Qadmu, see *RlA* 11, pp. 190–191, Qudma (Qudumu) and *ibid*., pp. 354–361, Richergott(heiten).

Line 41 *i*[*k*?-*ri*?-*bi*?]: My restoration is merely tentative. Based on the traces visible on MS G2 (K 3452+), one may restore here something like, *n*[*i-qi*] (for *nīqu*, 'offering, sacrifice') or *t*[*i-ni-ni*] (for *tīnīnu*, 'prayer'). *Malku* = *Šarru* V 78–86 equates *rēmu* or *rêmu* with *unnīnu*, *tīrānu*, *nakruṭu*, *naplusu*, *napšuru*, *tīnīnu*, *teslītum*, *epēqu*, *azāru*.[205] Given this connection, one can speculate that the ancients believed that prayers could elicit divine mercy.

Line 43 *sa-an-ni-nu*: LAMBERT 1960, p. 72 restored here *sap-ṣu* based on *Theodicy Commentary* obv 16. Yet, because we would expect here a word beginning with the sign *SA*, I have restored here *sa-an-ni-nu*, which is known from line 15 of the ancient commentary, and take *šap-ṣu* as its commentary, see OSHIMA, forthcoming.

---

198 HRŮŠA 2010, pp. 52–53.

199 *Ibid*., 138–139.

200 LAMBERT 1960, p. 54, line d.

201 OSHIMA, forthcoming.

202 LAMBERT, *ibid*., p. 72 and OSHIMA, forthcoming.

203 HRŮŠA 2010, pp. 78–79.

204 *RlA* 11, p. 190, Qudma.

205 HRŮŠA 2010, pp. 114–115.

Line 44 *l*]*i-bé-eš*: For the reading, I follow VON SODEN 1990, p. 149, note 44 a).[206]

Line 48 *ak-ka-an-nu sér-re-mu*: As already noted by LAMBERT 1960, p. 305, these Akkadian words in this particular line indicate the same animal although they normally denote two different animals in Akkadian texts. The distinction is clearly indicated by the fact that these animals are listed separately in the lexical list Ur$_5$-ra = *ḫubullu* XIII line 381a, dùr-AŠ.DU = *ak-ka-nu*; line 374, anše-eden-na = *sér-re-mu* following *imēru*, 'donkey,' and *sīsû*, 'horse'.[207]

Judging from the fact that one of the recurrent curse-formulae in the *Kudurru*-inscriptions damns the destroyer of the inscriptions to dwell outside the city or to roam the wilderness like an onager, it seems that, *serremu*, 'onager,' stood for the restlessness of the wild animal. Note, for example, ARNAUD 1972, p. 166, col. i, 39:[208]

39 ⌜*ki-ma*⌝ ANŠE.EDEN.NA (=*serremu*) *i-na ka-ma-ti li-ir-te-bi-iṣ*
39 Like an onager, may he always lie down outside.

Line 49 *ak-kat-ti-i pak-ki*: Given the entries in the *Theodicy Commentary*, *kat*$_6$-[*tu-u paq-q*]*i*$^?$: DÙ-*u*: MIN: *um-man-nu*,[209] it is evident that, with *kattī pakki*, the author alludes to *ummânu*, 'the scholar'.

Line 51: The priests utilized the *maṣḫatu*-flour both directly as burned offering and also as an ingredient for an offering cake, and so forth during different rituals and ceremonies in Mesopotamia. See, e.g., *CAD* M/1, pp. 330–331. However, it seems that, judging from the context, it is less likely that this line refers to such priestly activities but rather to the impious man's lack of willingness to participate or contribute to the cult activities.

According to the prayer to Šamaš recited during a dream ritual, a widow was expected to offer *maṣḫatu*-flour or a cake made of it while the rich people were required to bring lambs as offerings to the gods, lines 21–23 (BUTLER 1998, p. 274–275):

21 *na-šak-ka* DUMU ^{lú}ḪAL ^{giš}EREN
22 ^{f}*al-mat-tum ku-uk-ku-šú* ZÌ.MAD.GÁ *la-pu-un-tum* Ì+GIŠ *šá-ru-u*
23 *ina šá-ru-ti-šú na-ši pu-ḫa-du*

21 A diviner brings you cedar-(resin),
22 a widow (brings) a cake (v. omit) of *maṣḫatu*-flour, a poor woman (brings) oil, a rich man,
23 in his riches, carries a lamb.

Note also a parallel phrase in KAR 25, ii 19–20 (Syncretistic *Šuila*-prayer to Marduk).[210] Given the references to *maṣḫatu*-flour being a offering of widow in the prayer to Šamaš as well as the prayer to Marduk, one may argue that the *maṣḫatu*-flour symbolizes the most modest gift that a man can bring to the gods,

---

[206] This was already proposed in LANDSBERGER 1936, p. 48.
[207] MSL 8/1, p. 52.
[208] Note also ARNAUD 1972, p. 173, 64.
[209] LAMBERT 1960, p. 74.
[210] OSHIMA 2011, pp. 388–389, lines 17–18.

probably having the same meaning as the 'widow's mite' in English. That is to say that the sufferer is actually referring to the people who lack the decency to offer even the smallest goods to the gods.

Line 56 *iṣ-ṣi meš-re-e*: Literally, 'tree of wealth'. In cuneiform texts, this word is used as a descriptive name for the date palm. For example, an inscription of Sennacherib CT 26, pl. 27, col. vii lines 9b–10a (LUCKENBILL 1924, p. 109): *a-la-mit-ta* GIŠ *meš-re-e*, 'a palm tree, the wood of wealth.'[211] Note also that the lexical list Ur_5-ra = *ḫubullu* III, 274 equates giš-mu-níg-tuku,[212] a Sumerian word or Sumerogram, for the Akkadian *iṣ mešrê* – to *gišimmaru*, 'date palm'.

Line 57: VON SODEN 1990, p. 149, 57 a) also restores the last word: *u*[*r-ši*] and translates it "Klugheit."

Line 58 *gi-na-ta-ma*: VON SODEN 1990, p. 149 translates this word "winzig bist du." Note also his explanation in *ibid.*, note 58 a), "wörtlich »ein Kind«." On the other hand, I take *ginû* to be a Sumerian loan word from gi-na and an allusion to the correctness of the sufferer's argument although it primarily means 'regular, normal.' SELZ 2002, p. 163 best clarifies the concept behind it: "Er [i.e. the term níĝ-gi-na] bezeichnet den korrekten unabänderlichen Tatbestand, dann aber auch den Zustand der Welt, so wie er nach urzeitlichem Plan konzipiert ist, und d.h. so wie er eigentlich sein soll."[213] Incidentally, *a-ba-lu*, the last entry in the *Theodicy Commentary* line 23 for this word,[214] might be related to *a-ma-liš* from a sentence preserved in *Ludlul Commentary* rev 16. Although the *Ludlul Commentary* equates *a-ma-lu* with GIŠ.⸢Ù.SUḪ₅⸣, 'fir-tree,' *a-ma-liš* is used as a parallel of *ki-né-e*, 'mountain,' in this sentence.[215]

né-ṣú: My reading is based on BM 40098 (MS D). MS H (K 9290+9297) has *NI SI*. Unlike many other scholars, I tentatively take it to be the adjective *nēṣu*/*nēsu*, 'strong, great,' rather than the adjective/verb *nesû*, 'far' or 'to be/become far.' Most probably it is used as a synonym of *ginû*. To date, this word, *nēṣu*, is known only from lexical texts — e.g., Exp. Malku I 142: *nēṣu* (written *ne-e-ṣu*) = *gašru*, (with synonyms of *gašru*, 'strong');[216] and Exp. Malku I 31: *nēṣu* (written *ne-e-SU*) = *rubû*, (with synonyms of *rubû*, 'prince').[217]

This interpretation yields a better sense, particularly in connection with the word preceding it, *am-ma-tíš*, which until now has been an obstacle to understanding this line. While LANDSBERGER 1936, p. 51 and LAMBERT 1960, p. 75 take *am-ma-tíš* to be a part of the first verse, VON SODEN 1990, p. 149 interprets it to be an adverb belonging to the second portion of this line. FOSTER 2005, p. 916 follows von Soden's interpretation. The predicate of the second phrase is normal-

---

[211] = CT 26, pl. 27.

[212] MSL 5, p. 116.

[213] Note also SELZ 2008, p. 19, note 22: "[I]n Mesopotamia permanence has various positive connotations, as can be simply demonstrated by the use of the words gi-na // *kīnu*(*m*) "firm, permanent" as opposed to nu-gi-na / lul / lú-im // *sarru*(*m*) "unreliable; false, fraudulent.""

[214] LAMBERT 1960, p. 74.

[215] LAMBERT, *ibid.*, p. 54 line d. See also, VON SODEN 1956, p. 245.

[216] HRŮŠA 2010, pp. 158–159.

[217] *Ibid.*, pp. 150–151.

ly read as *ni-si* or *né-si*, (*nesû*, 'to be far'), yet as VON SODEN 1990, p. 149 note 58 b) questions, 'to be far like the earth' yields no clear sense. FOSTER 2005 made an additional attempt to understand this passage and offers a translation, "the purpose of the gods is remote as the netherworld." Because *Theodicy Commentary* line 23 explains the word *ammatiš* as GIM *er-ṣe-tú*, 'like the earth,' and the word *erṣetu* also indicates 'the netherworld,' Foster's interpretation is not absolutely impossible. On the other hand, I suggest taking *ammatu* to mean 'strong' based on *Malku = Šarru* I 51, which lists *ambatu* as a synonym of *dannātu* among the synonyms of *dannu*, *gāmeru*, and *gašru*.[218] According to this reading, it is very likely that *ammatiš* in this line of the *Babylonian Theodicy* likewise refers to firmness or strength rather than to distance. Note also the usage of *dannu*, literally 'strong,' in the sense of 'legitimate, reliable, regular', see *CAD* D, pp. 94, *dannu* 2.

Line 59 *gi-it-mul*: My restoration is based on MS F (BM 68589). LAMBERT 1960, p. 74 offered *gít-ma-lu* as the restoration of the beginning of this line based on *Theodicy Commentary* line 23. Yet, as it is clear from MS F, *gít-ma-lu* is a commentary for *gi-it-mul* just like *dan-nu* which follows *gít-ma-lu* in the commentary. The writing, *gi-it-mul* also better fits this section because we expect that each line should begin with the sign *GI* not the syllable <*gi*>. The form *gitmulu* is the infinitive of *gamālu* Gt-stem but, as the ancient commentary indicates, it functions like *gitmālu*, a derivative of the same root.

Line 60 *gi-mir*: The restoration is based on MS F (BM 68589). MS H has [*g*]*i*-⸢*mil*⸣, while the *Theodicy Commentary* preserves *gi-MI*[*S*: *g*]*a-ma*!*-ri*.[219] The first word of this line has been read *gi-iš* or *ge-iš* since LANDSBERGER 1936. Note, e.g., LAMBERT 1960, p. 74; *CAD* Q, p. 213, *qerbetu* 2 e); *CAD* R, p. 76, *raḫḫiṣu*; and PONCHIA 1996, p. 103. However, if my reading of *Theodicy Commentary* obv 24 is correct, it is very likely that [*g*]*i*-⸢*mil*⸣ (MS H) and *gi-MI*[*S*] of the commentary are scribal errors.

i-ḫaš-šú: For the reading of this word, I follow VON SODEN 1990, p. 150, note 60 b).

Line 61: One of the instructions credited to Šuruppak refers to a lion (an ED version 'dragon') as a thief, the *Instructions of Šuruppak*, § 30 (ALSTER 2005, p. 62):

> ní-zuḫ pirig̃[220] na-nam ul-dab₅ sag̃[221] na-nam
> The thief is a lion (when he was not caught); when he is caught, the thief is actually a slave.

This saying probably refers to the fact that when livestock are stolen, people tend to blame the theft on a lion, although it was in fact an act of a person (or a slave). It is hard to believe that the author of the *Babylonian Theodicy* had this phrase of the ancient sage Shuruppak in his mind, but this *Instruction of Shuruppak* certainly demonstrates the ancient perception of the lion saw the big cats not only in terms of their strength but also in terms of their thieving acts.

---

218 HRŮŠA 2010, pp. 32–33.

219 LAMBERT 1960, p. 74 and OSHIMA, forthcoming.

220 ED version, ušum, 'a dragon, python.'

221 ED version, g̃éme, 'slave-girl.'

Line 65: Judging from the contexts, it seems that *gerru*, 'path, way,' means 'way of life, behaviour' as well as 'terrible fate.' The use of *alāku*, 'to go,' which forms an idiom with *ana šimti*, literally, 'to go toward destiny', i.e., 'to die,' seems to be a word play and is designed to remind the reader of the premature death of people who gained their wealth without showing piety to the deities, as referred to above. Needless to say, this word rhymes with *gi-riš*, 'like the Fire-God,' in line 64 above.

Line 67 *iltānu*: LANDSBERGER 1936, p. 53 has already translated it "ein Nordwind." LAMBERT 1960, p. 75, and VON SODEN 1990, p. 150 follow him. FOSTER 2005, p. 917 probably follows their interpretation but gives the translation "cool breeze". Yet, one may also speculate that here a pun was intended between *iltānu*, 'northwind,' and *iltânu* (*ištênu*), 'one, first'.[222]

Line 68 *il-lu*: Very interestingly, *Malku* = *Šarru* IV 117 equates *illu*/*īltu* with *ṭēmu*.[223] A word meaning 'wisdom' or 'advice' would indeed fit well in the context, and one may take *il-lu* in this line of the *Babylonian Theodicy* to be a synonym of *ṭēmu*.[224]

Line 69: Literally, 'let me add one more word in front of you.'

Line 72: MS E adds *a-na* before *ṭè-em*.

Line 74 *né-me-li*: MS E (BM 47745) has *né-me-qú*. Because of similarity between *KU* (=*qú*) and *LU*, it is very likely a scribal error.

Line 76 *il-an-nu*: M. Streck kindly suggested to me taking the verb to be *le'û*, 'to be able, overcome,' instead of *elû*, 'ascend, rise.' Although his interpretation, "the crippled overcame me," yields a better sense in this context, I maintain *elû* because of the ancient commentary for this word, *il-an-ni* = *ana e-lu*, in *Theodicy Commentary* line 28. Note VON SODEN 1990, p. 150. Incidentally, LAMBERT 1960, p. 77 translates "my superior." The form preserved on MS H supports his interpretation. Needless to say, it is, of course, possible that the ancient commentator erroneously interpreted this word.

Line 77: Since the preposition *ana*, 'to,' yields no sense here, I take *a-na* to be a by-form of *anāku*, 'I,' which is mostly known from Old-Babylonian literary texts. See *GAG* § 41g. Yet, till now, *ana* for *anāku* is known only before the vowels *i* and *u*.

Line 78 *la mur-qa*: The *Theodicy Commentary* explains this word to be *la ṭe-⸢e⸣-*[*mu*], meaning 'without plan, reason.'[225] The interpretation 'reasonable thinking, rationality' for (*m*)*urqu*, literally 'green,' is already known from *Theodicy Commentary* line 12, the commentary on line 12: *ur-qa* = *ṭè-e-mu*.

Line 79 *ú-ṣur-ti*: The word *uṣurtu* normally means 'plan, line drawing' (of a figure, a building, constellations etc) but also the 'plans, order' of the gods. Howev-

---

[222] E.g., EBELING 1924, p. 9 translated, "Einzig".

[223] HRŮŠA 2010, pp. 100–101.

[224] However, the reconstruction of *illu*/*iltu* in *Malku* = *Šarru* is not certain, see *ibid.*, p. 244 commentary on IV 117.

[225] OSHIMA, forthcoming.

er, *Theodicy Commentary* line 30 equates *uṣurtu* with *parṣu*, '(divine)-office.'[226] My translation '*order*' for *uṣurtu* is meant to reflect the ancient commentary on this word.

Line 83 DINGIR *il-ti*: The reading is based on MS G4 (K 8463+). Although a word indicating 'goddess(es)' is expected here based on the pattern repeated in this poem, I take the term combination to mean 'god(s) and goddess(es)' instead of taking the sign DINGIR to be a determinative for *ilti*. The word *iltu* is also attested in line 86 but without the DINGIR sign before it on the same manuscript (K 8463+).

iš-še-[em-me: *CAD* Š/1, p. 32, *šadādu* 11 b) reads *iš-šad-da-ad ana libbi* by citing Lambert's unpublished manuscript. Note, however, *CAD* Q, p. 248, *qibītu* 5 d), *iššá[ddad ana libbi*], "are not taken seriously(?)." Despite these, I instead offer here *iš-še-[em-me*] based on MS G (1743+), because BM 47745 preserves *ḫa-a[s-*..., probably to be restored *ḫa-a[s-sa-at*].

Line 130 ^{d}*šà-s[ur*: The word *šasurru* means 'womb' and is often used as an epithet of the Mother-Goddess as is the case here in this line from the *Babylonian Theodicy*. For further discussions, see *RlA* 8, p. 507, Muttergöttin A. I., § 3.35; STOL 2000, pp. 77ff, esp. 80–83.

Line 136 *lu-kás*!-⌜*si*!-*is*!⌝: My reading is based on the collation.

Line 139 <*šar*>-*ra-qiš*: It is transliterated [*šar*]-*ra-qiš*. This word is preserved only on MS H. LANDSBERGER 1936, p. 56 has already suggested the emendation <*šar*>-*ra-qiš*, which has generally been accepted by various scholars including LAMBERT 1960, p. 78; *CAD* Š/2, p. 69, *šarraqiš*, a).

Line 141 *bi-ri-iš*: My translation is based on *bīru*, 'side, ridge.' VON SODEN 1990, p. 151 on the other hand, translates: "hungrig".

Line 142 *pí-is-nu-qiš*: The adjective *pisnuqu* means 'powerless, incapable.' Note, for example, the lexical list, MSL 14, 278, (A II/3) section E, 16'–18': $^{i\text{-}dím}$IDIM = *ú-la-lum, pi-is-na-qu, la le-ʾ-u*, 'IDIM = fool; powerless; not capable.' Note also the parallelism between *pisnuqu* and *enšu*, 'weak,' in *Prayer to Marduk no. 2*, line 13":[227]

13" *ta-zaq-qa-ap en-ša pi-is-nu-qa tu-rap-p[a-á]š*
13" You raise the weak, you stren[gth]en the feeble.

Line 148: My restoration is merely tentative. VON SODEN 1990, p. 152 148 a), on the other hand, reconstructs the first word: [*ib-ri-j*]*a-a-tu*, "Die Ge[fähr]ten-Menschen".

Line 177 *ma-a[l-l]e-e*: Given the fact that we would expect here an invocation addressed to the friend, *mallû* taken as another spelling for *malallû* (Sumerian má-lá), in the sense of 'raft,' is less likely. One could suggest the reading *ma-al le-e* for *mala lēʾi*, meaning 'as capable as,' but because, as yet, this line is only partial-

[226] LAMBERT 1960, p. 76.
[227] OSHIMA 2011, pp. 250–251.

ly preserved on but one manuscript (MS H), it is impossible to establish the exact reading.

Line 183: For the last word of this line, VON SODEN 1990, p. 152, note 183 a) offers a possible restoration: *i-š*[*aq-qal*], "dar[wägen]".

Line 184: VON SODEN 1990, p. 153, note 184 b) restores the last two words: *ṣ*[*u-bat muk-ki*], "ein Ge[wand aus Grober Wolle]".

Line 186 *uk-*[*lat-su*]: For the restoration of the last word, I follow, LAMBERT 1960, p. 80.

Line 187: VON SODEN 1990, p. 153, note 187 a) restores the last word: *t*[*a-tur-ru*], "Gewinn".

Line 198: VON SODEN 1990, p. 153 translates this line: "ein Gesetz seit jeher sind Reichtum ebenso wie Armut", see also note a) for line 198 on the same page.

Line 202 *ú-sa-an-di-i*: Very interestingly, the *Theodicy Commentary* explains *usandû*, 'fowler', as being equivalent to *ṭupšarru* 'scribe'.[228] Because the profession of a 'fowler' is in no way related to that of a 'scribe,' this entry should be taken to be an interpretation supplied by the ancient commentator. In other words, the author of the *Theodicy Commentary* understood *usandû*, 'fowler,' in this line as an allusion to the 'sufferer.' Note that *lāmi iṣṣūrī*, 'bird-catcher,' is also used as a reference to the protagonist, alias 'the scribe', in line 160 above.

ú-bí-lu: Given *Theodicy Commentary* rev 10': *ú-bí-lu = ba-ba-lu*: *na-da-nu*,[229] it is evident that the verb is not *belû*, D-stem, 'to destroy,' but (*w*)*abālu*, G-stem, 'to carry, bring.'

Line 206: Given the orthographies *-DA-an-ni* (MS E) and *-DA-ni* (MS G), we propose *paṭû*, in place of *petû* which is preferred by VON SODEN 1990, p. 153. Although *paṭû* has not been recorded in the dictionaries (namely *AHw*, *CAD* P, and *CDA*), according to *Malku = Šarru* V 95B, *paṭû* is a synonym of or a word related to *ḫadû*, 'to rejoice.'[230]

Line 207: At the end of the line, MS G1 has *pa*]*-ni-šú-un* instead, while MS E's *ana pa-ni-ia* is probably a scribal error.

Line 208 *ka-šá-me*: This is another form of *kīšāma*. *Malku = Šarru* III 109 lists *tušāma* as being its synonym.[231] Like *tušāma*, it appears to signify a false assumption or wrong perspective. For discussions of the meaning and its function, see HRŮŠA 2010, p. 234, note on *Malku = Šarru* III 109–122; *ibid* p. 276, note on VIII 114; KREBERNIK and STRECK 2001, pp. 67–71, esp. 67; WASSERMAN 2002. Taking *kašāme* as a variant of *tušāma* better fits the context than the other interpretations offered by other scholars, e.g., *AHw*, p. 490, "verzeih mir!" and *CAD* K, p. 445, *kīša* b), "evidently." For *kīšāma*, cf. also the explanation of *kīma ša* on KREBERNIK and STRECK *op. cit.*, p. 72.

---

[228] OSHIMA, forthcoming.

[229] LAMBERT 1960, p. 82.

[230] HRŮŠA 2010, pp. 116–117.

[231] *Ibid.*, pp. 82–83.

Line 210 ⸢*ḫa*!-*áš*!⸣-*šá-mu-u*: This word is preserved only on MS E. Because *ḫaššamû*, probably a variant of *ḫaššāʾu*. 'cripple,' does not yield a good sense, one may speculate that it is a scribal error for *ḫiššamû*, 'splendid, superb.' If so, this line should be translated: "[*For* ...] the superb chariot of the king turned [around]."

Line 211 *ḫur-sa-an-*[*nu*]: For *ḫursānu*/*ḫursannu* = *šadû*, note, *Malku* = *Šarru* II 36.[232] One may also take it for *ḫursānu*, 'river-ordeal.'

Line 212: Literally, 'You make your clear heart possess errancy.'

Line 215 *šúḫ-ḫu-ú*: LAMBERT 1960, p. 82 restores *bu-*[*b*]*í-nu* before *šaḫ-ḫu-ú*, most likely based on the word attested before the sign *SAG* in *Theodicy Commentary* rev 16'. On the other hand, also taking the word preserved in *Theodicy Commentary* rev 16' to be the main entry, VON SODEN 1990, p. 154 and note 215 a), reads the same word *bu-*[*k*]*a-nu* and translates this line: "[...] die Übergabestäbe sind unkenntlich gemacht, fern von ihm ist der Ziegelkorb." Based on the collation with *Theodicy Commentary* rev 16' and the new copy, however, I read ⸢*šu-uḫ-ḫu*⸣: *pu-*[*ut-t*]*u-nu* instead of Lambert's *bu-*[*b*]*í-nu* and von Soden's *bu-*[*k*]*a-nu*. In other words, *pu-*[*ut-t*]*u-nu* is most probably a commentary on *šuḫḫu* and not the main entry. If my interpretation of *Theodicy Commentary* rev 16' is correct, it is very likely that the ancient commentator took *šuḫḫu* (probably the D-stem of *šâḫu*, 'to grow') to be a synonym of *puttunu*, D-stem of *patānu*, 'to be/become strong.' Yet, due to the lacuna in the beginning of the line, the overall meaning of this phrase is still unclear.

Line 217: Given the context, the acrostic and the rhyme, I restore here *ri-it-pa-šu* ŠÀ-*bu*, 'his mind is wide (i.e., he is talented),' as a possible reconstruction of the beginning of this line. Note ŠÀ-*ba rit-pa-šu* in line 234 below. For this expression, also note, although it has *karšu*, a synonym *of libbu* instead, *Bull Inscription* line 4 (LUCKENBILL 1924, p. 117): *ù* ᵈ*nin-ši-ku id-di-na kar-šú* (v. *-šu*) *rit-pa-šu*, 'and Ninšiku (=Ea) gave me a wide mind (i.e., wisdom).' Incidentally, *Theodicy Commentary* rev 17' preserves *le-ʾ-u*[233] which, given the sequence of the words, is most likely a commentary on the first word of this line.

pa[*l*]*-ku-u*: Like *mūdû*, 'knowledgeable, wise,' in line 201 (*Commentary* rev 9') and *usandû*, 'fowler,' in line 202 (*Commentary* rev 10'), *Theodicy Commentary* rev 17' explains *palkû* to be *ṭup-šar-ri*,[234] i.e., it is an allusion to the sufferer alias scribe.

Line 220: The restoration is merely tentative. Judging from the context, words meaning 'to drive away, abandon, disregard' would be expected here.

Line 224 *ḫu-bu*[*r*: Judging from *Theodicy Commentary* rev 20': *ḫu-bu-ru* = *ši-kar* = *šá-niš* × [..., 'beer, beer-jar = beer = secondly . [...,'[235] *ḫu-bu*[*r* in this line is not the Hubur-river but a beer or beer-jar.

---

[232] *Ibid.*, pp. 54–55.

[233] LAMBERT 1960, 82.

[234] *Ibid.*

[235] *Ibid.*, p. 84.

Line 226 *ta-bi-na*: This is also restored on the basis of the entries in *Theodicy Commentary* rev 22'[236] although its ancient explanation is not preserved.

Line 234 *ni-×-šu*: LAMBERT 1960, p. 84 reads, *ni-⸢ip⸣-šu*. Note also, *CAD* N/2, p. 248, *nipšu* A, 1. Due to the poor preservation of VAT 10567, I could not confirm their reading.

Line 236: The first word of the line, *ša*(-)*am-mé-e*, whose exact reading has not yet been established, poses a difficulty in interpreting the entire line. It is clear from the context that this word indicates possession or even wealth paralleling *bunašu*, 'his goodness,' from line 235 above. *CAD* Š/1, p 321, for example, takes it as *šammû* and suggests that the word should mean something like "agility" or "grace" based on the context.

Line 242 MU.AN.NA: For MU.AN.NA (=*šattu*) as 'a harvest time,' instead of its more common meaning 'year,' see the commentary on line 272 below.

Line 244 *šar-ra-bi*: A god-list, CT 25, 36, identifies ^{d}*šar-ra-bu* to be ^{d}*lugal-gìr-ra* MAR.KI, 'Lugal-girra of MAR.KI,' (rev 30 // *ibid.*, 35, rev 24 // *ibid.*, 37, obv 20). Lugalgirra is one of the divine Twins (the second god is Meslamtaea[237]). Likewise, the god-list An=*Anum* lists ^{d}KAL$^{ša\text{-}ra\text{-}ab}$EDIN as a member of ^{d}*maš-tab-ba* (the Twins: Lugalgirra and Meslamtaea) circle (An=*Anum* V, 304 and 309).[238] An ancient catalogue of hymns to different deities lists *it-ta-ṣi* ^{d}*šar-ra-bu be-lu a-nu-na-ti*, 'Šarrabu, the lord of battles, went forth,' clearly it was the incipit of a hymn to the god, (KAR 158, i 23). For further discussions on Šarrabu, see *RlA* 12, pp. 70–71, Šarrabu.

Line 246 ^{giš}*dun-ni*: For the meaning of *dunnu* as 'a bed,' note *Malku* = *Šarru* II 190: *dunnu* = *majjaltu*, '*cot* = bed.'[239] The same entries are also attested in exp. *Malku*= *Šarru* III 371.[240]

Line 255 DINGIR *ta-da-a-aṣ*: Literally, 'you treat the divine with disrespect.'

Line 258 ^{d}*a-ru-ru*: Aruru is a name of the Mother-Goddess(es), see *RlA* 8, p. 504, Müttergöttin A. I., § 3.3.

Line 259 *mur-ri*: *Malku* = *Šarru* IV 124 interprets *murrû* to mean *qâl*[*u*] *ša aw*[*āti*]. HRŮŠA 2010, p. 101 translates *qâl*[*u*] *ša aw*[*āti*] "schweigen, in Bezug auf Wort," while he translates *murrû* "verstummen (das Word, 'langsam machen' oder 'abschneiden'?)," on p. 101 probably following *AHw*, p. 1497, *wurrûm*. Note also VON SODEN 1990, p. 155, who, taking it to be *wurrû*, "abschneiden, abtrennen, unterbrechen,' thus translates *Babylonian Theodicy* 259: "warum ist da allenthalben ein Abkömmling nicht (richtig) abgenabelt?" He further notes: "Wer nicht richtig abgenabelt wurde, wurde bei der Geburt nicht angemessen versorgt und war daher im späteren Leben oft kränklich. Vgl. dazu, *AHw*, S. 1497 s.v.

---

[236] *Ibid.*

[237] For these divine twins, see *RlA* 7, pp. 143–145.

[238] LITKE 1998, pp. 197–198.

[239] HRŮŠA 2010, pp. 66–67.

[240] *Ibid.*, pp. 192–193.

wurrûm," *ibid*., pp. 155–156, note 259 a). FOSTER 2005, p. 920, in addition, offers "unmatched," as a possible translation of this word.

On the other hand, I take the above mentioned *qâl*[*u*] *ša aw*[*āti*] to mean 'heeding of word,' i.e. 'to listen to speech, to be attentive,' because the verb *qâlu* is very frequently used with the sense, 'to hear,' when it is attested with words like *qibītu*, *qabû*, *zikru*, and *awatu*, all meaning, 'speech, word.' For this interpretation, see *CAD* Q, pp 73–74, *qâlu* 2 a)–b). Therefore, I suggest 'attentive' as the most likely meaning of *murrû*.

Line 269: VON SODEN 1990, p. 156 and note 269 a), following BIGGS 1969, p. 604, offers the restoration, *k*[*it-tú*], "Wahr[heit]," for the last word of this line. See also *CAD* A/2, p. 153, *ananzilu* a). However, *kittu*, 'justice,' does not yield good sense here. Note, for example, *ibid*: "the evildoer for whom that which should be an abomination to him is right." More crucially, the sign after *ŠÚ* begins with a short horizontal stroke which cannot be *KID* by any means.

Line 271 *pa-šal-lu*: Because *Theodicy Commentary* 32' equates *pa-šal-la* with *ḫu*-[*r*]*a-ṣu*, 'gold,'[241] it is evident that *pašallu* is related to a particular kind of gold. Note that *Malku* = *Šarru* V, 168 also refers to *pašallu* among other words indicating certain types of gold.[242]

Line 272 *iš-pik-ku*: The *Theodicy Commentary* explains *išpikku*, 'grain-bin,' to be Ì.D[UB] = MU.AN.NA = *la kit-tú*.[243] While Ì.DUB is a common Sumerogram for *išpikku*, MU.AN.NA normally stands for *šattu*, 'year.' Therefore, one finds no obvious semantic connection between these entries. Here I take MU.AN.NA (*šattu*) to be 'harvest time' rather than 'year,' probably it is used to connote 'income' or 'profit' because *lā šattu*, literally 'no harvest (time),' is explained as *lā kušīru*, 'no success, profit,' in CT 41, 27, rev 28 (*Ālu Comm*.). Note also line 242 of the *Babylonian Theodicy* and *Theodicy Commentary* rev 24' above.

Line 276 ^{d}*nar-ru*: As is clear from the entry ^{d}*na-ar-ri* = ^{d}*en-líl* in *Theodicy Commentary* rev 34', Narru is Enlil, not Nāru, 'the Divine-River.' See, *RlA* 6, p. 495, Larru (Narru). Incidentally, HUROWITZ 2004, pp. 777–778, related this DN to the Akkadian word, *narru*, which *Malku* = *Šarru* I 88 takes to be a synonym of *sāru*, 'false, criminal.'[244] By taking su-lum-mar as being an Akkadian equivalent of *ṭupullû*, meaning 'Schähmung, Verdächtigung,' he further explains in this article that Zulammar in the following line also indicates 'lie.' For su-lum-mar = *ṭupullû*, see *AHw*, p. 1396, *ṭupullû*.

Line 277 ^{d}*zu-lum-ma-ru*: A god list (CT 25, 33, K 4209, line 16) refers to ^{d}*DU*$_{11}$^{zu}*-lum-GAR*^{mar} as being another name of the god Ea. The *Theodicy Commentary* explains that ^{d}*su-l*[*um-ma*]*r* is Ea (^{d}IDIM) who bears *wellness* (*šá šá-lum-tú na-šu-ú*). For the ancient commentary, see LAMBERT 1960, p. 88 and OSHIMA, forthcoming. It seems that with the term *šá-lum-tú*, the commentator

241 The *Theodicy Commentary* further explains that *pašallu* is related to *ana pa-šá-lu*, 'to crawl.' It appears to be some sort of wordplay but the exact sense behind it escapes us. LAMBERT 1960, p. 87.

242 HRŮŠA 2010, pp. 118–119.

243 OSHIMA, forthcoming.

244 HRŮŠA 2010, pp. 36–37.

meant *šalmūtu* not *šullumtu*, i.e. 'completion, final payment' because he further explains the word to be *su-lim* = *šá-l[um-m]a-tum*. The additional gloss MAR = GAR = *na-šú-u* suggests that the commentator understood the name to be an Emesal Sumerian word.

Line 285: I follow the interpretation of VON SODEN 1990, p. 157, "Bösartig packen sie ihm jegliches Übel auf, weil er der Führung ermangelt." Cf. also, FOSTER 2005, p. 921: "They make him suffer every evil because he has no wherewithal(?)."

Lines 288–292: MS A (BM 34633) preserves a divergent order of lines:

A iv 10' = 289	*re-ši-šú pal-ḫu-át mut-nin-nu-ú a-na-⸢ku⸣*
A iv 11' = 291	*re-bit* URU-*iá a-ba-ʾu né-ḫi-iš*
A iv 12' = 292	*ri-ig-mu ul iš-šá-pu šá-pil at-mu-⸢ú-a⸣*
A iv 13' = 288	*ri-ŠÁ-am nam-[r]a-ṣu a-mur lu-ú ti-i-du*
A iv 14' = 290	*ri-ṣa tuk-lat za-mar u ul a-mur*

Judging from the shape, it seems that the sign *ŠÁ* in A iv 13' is an error for *ṣa* (the scribe forgot to write an additional vertical stroke).

Line 288 *ri-ṣa-am*: Based on *Theodicy Commentary* rev 37': [*ri-ṣa-a*]*m-ma* = *ra-a-ṣa* = *a-lak šá-niš* DAḪ = *r*[*a-a-ṣa*], 'come to help me = to come to help = to go = secondly the sign *DAḪ* = to c[ome to help],'[245] one may suggest taking this word to be the imperative of *râṣu*, 'rush (to help)', rather than of *rêṣu*, 'to help,' as has generally been assumed, e.g., *AHw* p. 972, *rêṣu*.[246]

Line 289 *re-e-šú*: VON SODEN 1990, p. 157 translates this line: "Ein Sklave, der viel weiß und viel betet, bin ich." But judging from the orthography *re-ši-šú* on MS A, it seems that this word actually indicate 'head' rather than 'servant.'

pal-ku-ú: MS A preserves *pal-ḫu-át* instead.

Line 292 *ri-ig-mu ul iš-šá-pu iš-šá-pil at-mu-ú-a*: When the verb *šapû* in the G-stem is used in order to describe the state of voice or sound, it normally means 'to be/become loud, sonorous.' Given that, it is very likely that *šapālu* in the second sentence means 'to be lowered' as in English (e.g., to lower the voice), providing a more precise meaning than the vague translation 'to be humble.' Note LAMBERT 1960, p. 89: "My voice was not raised, my speech was kept low."[247]

Line 293: One may compare this line to Aššurnaṣirpal's prayer to Ištar of Nineveh, lines 69–70 (VON SODEN 1974–77, p. 42):

69 IGI.MIN-*a-a bit-ru-ma* «*ma*» *ul ú-ṣab-ba-a* […]
70 *ul ú-šá-qa-a a-na e-le-ni pa-an qaq-qa-ri* [*a*?-*na*?-*ṭa*?-*al*?]

69 My eyes stare but cannot see […],
70 I cannot raise (the eyes) high, [I stare at] the surface of the ground.

re-ši-ia ul ul-lu: Cf. the expressions like *rēšu našû*, 'to raise one's head,' or its nominal form, *nīš rēši*. One may compare this line with *Ludlul* I, 73:

---

[245] LAMBERT 1960, p. 88.

[246] However, we normally expect *rūṣ* for the imperative of this verb.

[247] Note also similar translations by FOSTER 2005, p. 921; and VON SODEN 1990, p. 157.

73 *šá-qa-a-tum re-šá-a-a ik-nu-uš qaq-qar-šun*
73 My head which used to be held high bowed down to the ground

As already discussed in the introductory section, 'to raise one's head,' has three different meanings: 'to be/become proud of,'[248] 'to pay attention to, to heed,'[249] and 'to save/be saved.'[250] On the other hand, the second sentence in this line, 'I star[e] at the ground (i.e., keeps his head down),' probably signifies either the depression/despair of the sufferer or the humiliation imposed on him.

Line 296 *i*[*z-ba-an-ni*]: My restoration is based on *Theodicy Commentary* rev 38': [*iz-ban-ni* =] ⌜*e*$^{?}$⌝-*zeb* = *na-par-ku-u* = *ba-ṭa-lu*, '[she left me =] to leave = to abandon = to cease,'[251] although the *Commentary* does not preserve the main entry itself but only its infinitive form and synonyms. For a parallel, see *Ludlul* I, 43–44:

43 *id-da-an-ni* DINGIR-MU *šá-da-a-šú i-li*
44 *ip-par-ku* ^{d}*iš-ta-ri i-bé-eš a-ḫi-tum*

43 My god abandoned me and disappeared,
44 my goddess deserted (me) and moved away.

Line 297: Various scholars take ^{d}UTU-*ši ni-ši* to be a single unit and thus translate "the sun of the people" (e.g., LANDSBERGER 1936, p. 73; BIGGS 1969, p. 604; LABAT 1970, p. 327; and VON SODEN 1990, p. 157). However, LAMBERT 1960, p. 89 and FOSTER 2005, p. 922 take ^{d}UTU-*ši* to be the divine name of Šamaš, the Sun-God. Yet, if my restoration of the last word of this line, *li-saḫ-ḫ*[*ir*], is correct, none of these interpretations can be supported, and ^{d}UTU-*ši* should be read *šamšī*, 'my Sun.' But then we must ask, who is this 'the shepherd, my Sun'?

As we know from personal names consisting of *šamšī* with DNs, e.g., *šamšī-adad*, 'My-Sun-is-Adad', ^{d}UTU-*ši* in the *Babylonian Theodicy* can be another deity other than Šamaš himself. Note, for example, Marduk's title in *Enūma Eliš* I 101–102: *ma-ri-ú-tu ma-ri-ú-tu ma-ri* ^{d}UTU-*ši* ^{d}UTU-*ši šá* DINGIR.DINGIR, "Mariutu, Mariutu, the Son of the Sun, the Sun of the gods.' Cf., *Enūma Eliš* VI 127: *lu-ú ma-ru* ^{d}UTU-*ši šá* DINGIR.DINGIR *né-bu-ú-šu-ma*, 'May his (Marduk's) name be the Son of the Sun of the gods!'[252] As a divine epithet, see *CAD* Š/1, p. 337, *šamšu* 1 e) 1' b'–3'. Given the personal names like *šamšī-ilu* and *samsu-iluna*, it is also possible that this word refers to the personal gods. Such an interpretation seems reasonable, particularly because the previous lines most probably refer to the personal gods of the sufferer.

LANDSBERGER 1936, p. 73 and VON SODEN 1990, p. 157, note 297 a) suggest that a human king is intended. STOL 1996, p. 183 note 11, referring to line 64 that speaks of the king's punishments of malevolent people, also suggests that this line refers to the human king. In fact, Sumerian utu and Akkadian *šamšu*, 'the Sun', are frequently attested as epithets of kings. For example, the legendary king En-

---

[248] E.g., *Ludlul* I 73.

[249] E.g., *Ludlul* II 5.

[250] E.g., *Ludlul* V 11. Note also, *CAD* N/2, p 108, *našû* A, 6 with *rēšu* d) and *ibid.*, p 297, *nīšu* B, 5.

[251] OSHIMA, forthcoming.

[252] HUROWITZ 2010, pp. 89–90 calls it a "name-midrash."

merkar is ᵈutu-kalam-ma, 'the Sun of the land',[253] while Hammurabi of Babylon called himself in *Codex Hammurabi* v 4–9: *šamaš bābilim mušēṣi nūrim ana māt šumerim u akkadim*, 'the Sun/Sun-god of Babylon, the one who spreads the light over the land of Sumer and Akkad.'[254] Further, the Assyrian kings, e.g., Tukluti-Ninurta I[255] and Šalmanesser III[256], very often used the royal title *šamaš kiššat nišē*, 'the Sun/Sun-god of the entire people,' in their inscriptions.[257]

When the Assyrian king Esarhaddon suffered depression, his chief exorcist, Adad-šumu-uṣur, sent him a letter to encourage him. In this letter, he refers to the king as the Sun-God, Šamaš, SAA 10, no. 196, obv 17–rev 6:

> *a-na* ᵈUTU LUGAL DINGIR.MEŠ *man-nu* ⌜*id-du-ru*⌝ *u₄-mu k*[*al*] ⌜*mu-ši*⌝ *e-da-ar tu-ú-ra ši-it-ta ú-ma-ti* LUGAL EN KUR.KUR *ṣa-al-mu šá* ᵈUTU *šu-ú mi-ši-il u₄-me ú-ta-da-ar*

> Who stays in the dark longer than Šamaš, the king of the gods? (Who) stays in the dark a day and whole night, and again another night? The king, the lord of the lands, is the image of Šamaš. He (should) stay in the dark for half a day (alone)!

Moreover, note the personal names consisting of *šamšī*, 'my Sun,' with RNs, e.g., *šamšī-šulgi*, 'Šulgi-is-My-Sun'; *šamšī-ḫammurapi*, 'Hammurabi-is-My-Sun,' and so forth.[258] In addition, the Sumerian word utu, 'the Sun', is also used as a title of human kings, see Seux 1967, p. 460.

One may also refer to *Ludlul* I, line 55:

55 LUGAL UZU DINGIR.DINGIR ᵈUTU *šá* UN.MEŠ-*šú*
55 The king, the flesh of gods, the sun of his people

Given a very common royal title, *rēʾû*, 'shepherd,'[259] which probably designates the ability (and duty) of a human king to lead people correctly and righteously, as well as the last word of the acrostic, *šarri*, 'of king,' it is almost certain that with this *rēʾû šamšī*, 'the shepherd, my Sun,' the author is referring to the human king.

li-saḫ-ḫ[*ir*]: It is restored from the last entry of the *Theodicy Commentary* (rev 38').[260] Although ⌜*e*⌝-*zeb*: *na-par-ku-u*: *ba-ṭa-lu* of rev 38' of the commentary

---

[253] The *Enmerkar and Lord of Arata*, line 309, (Mittermayer 2009, pp. 132 and 261–267).

[254] Roth 1995, p. 80.

[255] RIMA 1, p. 244, 3.

[256] RIMA 3, p. 7, 2; p. 13, 5.

[257] For other examples of this epithet, see Seux 1967, pp. 283–294. The motif of Assyrian kings being the Sun/Sun-god, see Maul 1999, p. 206. Note also, Beckman 2002.

[258] For these PNs, see, Seux 1967, p. 283 note 108.

[259] *Ibid.*, pp. 244–250. For the motif of the king as the shepherd of mankind as a whole, see Selz 2001; Goodnick-Westenholz 2004. Incidentally, Brinkman 1974, p. 405 notes that *rēʾû*, 'shepherd,' is the most common epithet of the Kassite kings. This fact probably speaks in favour of a late second millennium dating for the *Babylonian Theodicy* as I discussed above in the introduction.

For the role of Šamaš as the one who bestows shepherdship on the human king, note, Assurbanipal's coronation hymn, SAA 3, no. 11, 1:

1 ᵈUTU LUAGL AN-*e u* KI-*tim a-na* SIPA-*u*[*t kib-r*]*at erbe-tim liš-ši-ka*
1 May Šamaš the king of the heavens and the earth, elevate you to the shepherdship over the four [region]s.

[260] Oshima, forthcoming.

could still be a commentary for *šá id-dan-ni*, 'who have forsaken me,' (= line 295), there is no suitable word for *li-saḫ-ḫ*[*ir*] in lines 296–297.[261]

[261] MS A (BM 34633) also preserves some traces of a sign after *i-liš*. Judging from the remaining traces, however, that sign cannot be *IR* or *NI* as Lambert copied, but must rather be *LIŠ*. Perhaps the text should be read *l*[*is-saḫ-ḫir*]?

GLOSSARY AND INDICES

Logograms and Their Readings

AN → *šamû;*
DINGIR → *ilu, ilūtu;*
EDIN → *ṣēru;* EN → *bēlu;*
GIŠ.MÁ → *eleppu;*
KUR.NU.GI_4 → *kurnugû;*
LUGAL → *šarru;*
MU.AN.NA → *šattu;* MUŠEN → *iṣṣūru;*
NAM.LÚ.U_{18}.LU → *amēlūtu;* NUN → *rubû;*
ŠÀ → *libbu;* ŠU → *qātu;*
UD → *ūmu;* UKKIN → *puhru;* UN → *nīšū;* UR.MAH → *nēšu*

Glossary

abālu "to bring": *ub-bal* 125, *ub-lam* 144, *ú-bil* 51, *ú-bil-lu* 202,

abātu "to destroy, (N) to flee": *ib-ba-tu* 274,

abšānu "yoke, harness": *ab-šá-nu* 74,

abu "father": *ab-bu-nu* 16, *a-bi* 11,

adnāti "world, people": *ad-na-a-ti* 243,

agarinnu "womb, mother": *a-ga-rin-nu* 10,

aggu "angry": *ag-gu* 50,

agû "high wave, flood water": *a-g[a-a]* 138,

ahāzu "to seize, understand, learn": *a-ta-haz* 45, *lu-hu-uz* 137, *šu-hu-za* 86, *[š]u-hu-za* 204, *šu-hu-zu-šú* 285,

ahu "brother": *a-hi* 56, 247,

ahurrû "junior, younger child": *a-hu-ra-[k]u-ma* 9, *a-hu-ru-ú* 253,

ai "lest, shall not": *a-a* 134, 165,

aiu "which?": *a-a-ú* 161,

ajjāna "where?": *a-a-na* 5,

ajjiš "where, whither": *a-a-iš* 6,

akalu "food, bread": *a-kal-šú* 240, *ak-lu* 136,

akālu "to eat": *i-tak-ka-lu* 50,

akāšu "to go, walk": *i-ku-šu* 65,

akkannu "wild ass": *[ak]-ka-an-nu* 48,

akkâta "to you": *ak–ka-ta* 47,

alādu "to give birth": *i-al-lad* 262,

alaktu "way, behaviour, divine decree": *a-lak-ta* 244, *a-lak-ta-šú* 33, *a-l[ak-ti]* 25,

alāku "to go; (Š) to make suitable, appropriate": *a-la-ka* 65, *il-la-ku* 16, 70, 282, *lu-ul-lik* 137, *t[u-šá-lik]* 37,

ali "where?": *a-[li* 7,

ālittu "mother, begetter": *a-lit-ti* 10,

ālu "city": URU-*ia* 291,

amāru "to see, experience": *a-mur* 288, 290,

amatu "word": *a-mat* 267,

amēlu "man": *a-me-lu* 283,

amēlūtu "mankind": *a-me-lut-ti* 279, NAM.[LÚ].U$_{18}$.[LU 149,

ammatiš "like a land": *am-ma-tíš* 58,

amû "to tell, speak": *lu-ú-ta-me-šú* 7,

ana "to, for": *ana* 80, 85, 142, 209, 216, 227, 231, 279, *a-na* 26, 31, 41, 53, 159, 220, 242, 244, 250,

ana B "I": *a-na* 77,

ana surri "immediately": *a-na sur-ri* 26, 242,

anāku "I": *a-na-a-ku* 289, *a-na-ku* 252, *[a-na-ku]* 4,

annu "crime": *an-n[u]* 273,

annû "this": *an-nu-tu-ú* 65,

anzillu "abomination, taboo": *an-zil-la-šú* 269,

apātu "numerous; epithet of mankind": *a-pa-a-t[um]* 18, 276, *a-pa-a-[tú]* 84,

aplu "son, heir": *ap-lum* 249,

appu "nose": *ap-pi* 73,

aqru "valuable, rare": *aq-ra-a* 53, *aq-ri* 46, *aq-r[u]* 56,

aqû "to wait": *ú-taq-qam-ma* 265,

arāku "to be(come) long; (Š) to lengthen": *šu-ru-uk* 191,

arku "long": *ar-ka-tu* 126,

arkû "second, junior, rear, later": *ar-ku-ú* 261,

aṣābu "to add": *uṣ-ṣu-bu-šú* 52,

āšišu "wise": *a-š[i]š* 1,

ašpaltu "social inferior": *áš-pal-ti-ia* 252,

ašru "humble": *áš-ru* 166,

aššaru "expert": *áš-šá-ru* 167,

aššu "because": *áš-šú* 285,

ašû "living creatures": *a-šu-ú* 162,

atāru "to be additional": *ú-at-tar* 251,

atmû "speech, words": *at-mé-e-a* 266, *at-[mé-e-ka]* 46, *at-mu-ú-a* 292,

atû "to find": *ut-tu-ú* 165,

bâ'u "to come, go": *a-ba-'u-ú* 291,

bahû "to be(come) thin": *ba-hi* 240,

bal "without": *ba-al* 11,

bâlu "to supplicate; supplication": *b[a-a-li]* 40,

bāntu "mother": *ba-an-ti* 11, 159,

banû "to build, create": *ba-nu-ú* 276,

banû B "to be(come) beautiful; (D) to care of": *[u]b-te-en-ni* 128,

barû "to look, observe": *ab-re-e-ma* 243, *bit-r[i]* 61,

bašû "to be, exist": *ba-a-ši* 218, *ib-š[i]* 49, *[i]b-šu-ú* 146,

batāqu "to cut off": *[ib-ba-t]aq-ma* 150,

baṭālu "to cease": *ba-ṭi-il* 29,

behēru "to select": *[u]b-te-eh-hir* 130,

belû "to be extinguished, end; (D) to bring to an end, destroy, extinguish": *[u]b-tel-li* 127, *ú-bal-lu-šú* 286,

bēl pāni "wealthy man" EN–*pa-an* 52, 63, *be-el–pa-ni* 275,

bēlu "lord, master, owner": *be-el* 275, *be-lu* 20, 124, EN 52, 63, 187, [E]N 5,

bēru "bull calf; hunger, thirst": *bé-e-ra* 136,

bēru B "distant" *bé-e-ra* 139,

bēšu "far apart, distant": *bé-e-šú* 143,

bêšu "to go away": *l]i-bé-eš* 44,

bīri "among": *bi-ri-šú-nu* 163,

bīriš "over, to the other side": *bi-ri-iš* 141,

birītu "space between, distance": *bi-ir-ta* 137,

bīru "baulk, ridge between fields, canals" *bé-e-ra* 138,

bīšu "possession, property": *bi-šá-a* 134,

bītbītiš "from house to house": *bi-it-bi-ti-iš* 140,

bītu "house, estate": *bi-i-ta* 133,

bu''û "to seek": *lu-ba-'i* 164, *tu-ba-'u-ú* 239, *ub-te-e'-u* 132,
bubūtu "hunger": *bu-bu-ti* 140,
bukru "son, first-born": *bu-kúr* 19, *bu-kúr-šu* 246,
bullu "to throw, strike down": *bu-ul-la-ak* 231, *ub-til* 9,
būltu see *būštu,*
būlu "animals, livestock": *bu-li* 61,
būnu "goodness": *bu-na-šu* 235,
buqlu "malt": *bu-uq-li* 183,
būru "calf": *bu-ur-šu* 260,
būštu "shame": *bu-ul-tum* 229,
būšu "property": *bu-šá* 223,
dabābu "talk; to talk": *da-ba-ba* 279, *da-b]a-bu* 46, *i-dab-bu-bu* 281,
dalālu "to praise": *a-dal-lal* 294, *lud-lul-ka* 4,
damāqu "to be(come) favourable, good": *ú-dam-mi-iq-šú* 20,
damāṣu "to humble": *ad-da-mu-ṣu* 251,
damqu "favourable, fine, good": *da-mi-iq-ti* 220, *d[am-qu]* 68,
danānu "to be(come) strong, hard": *ú-dan-na-nu* 273,
darāsu "to trample over, push": *i-dar-ri-is-su* 274,
dārû "everlasting": *da-ra-a* 66,
dâṣu "to treat unjustly, with disrespect": *ta-da-a-aṣ* 255,
dubbubiš "into incoherent speech": *dub-bu-biš* 35,
dumqu "favour, wellness": *dum-qí* 33, 70, *dum-qí-šú* 281, *dum-qu* 143, *du-muq* 50, *du-um-qí* 66, *du-un-qí-ma* 208,
dunnamû "person of lowly status, pitiable": *dun-na-ma-a* 268, 283,
dunnu "power, strength; a type of bed": GIŠ.*dun-ni* 246,
duppussû "younger son": *dup-pu-šu-ú* 248,
ebēru "to cross": *eb-bé-ri* 17,
edlu "locked up": *ed-lu-tú* 207,
edû see *idû,*
eleppu "boat, ship": GIŠ.MÁ 245,
elēṣu "to swell, rejoice": *i-li-iṣ-ma* 248,
elû "to be(come) high; (D) to raise, lift up": *il-an-nu* 76, *ul-lu* 293,
emēdu "to impose": *te-te-mid* 36,
emēqu "(Št) to pray devoutly": *muš-te-mi-qu* 71,
emû "to change": *tu-še-e-ma* 15,
enēšu "to be(come) weak, poor": *i-te-en-šú* 71, *i-te-niš* 29,
enqu "wise": *en-qu* 206,
enšu "poor, weak": *en-šú* 19,
epēšu "to do": *i-pu-šu* 62,
epištu "deed": *[ep-š]á-a-tú* 148,
erēbu "to enter": *lu-ter-ru-ba* 140, *lu-t[er-ru-ba* 142,
erqu "green, vegetable": *er-qu* 185,
eṣēpu see *aṣābu,*
ešēru "to be(come) straight": *i-ši-ri* 8, *šu-te-šu-ru* 41,
etēqu "to pass by": *e-te-ti-iq* 28, *te-te-eq* 81,
etguru "crossed over, intertwined": *et-gu-ru* 279,
etnušu "very weak, poor": *et-nu-šu* 275,
ezēbu "to leave, abandon, forsake": *i[z-ba-an-ni]* 296, *i-zi-ba* 165, *i-zi-bu-in-ni-ma* 11,
gamālu "to do a favour, spare, be favourable": *gi-it-mul* 59,
gamāru "to destroy, finish": *a-ga-m[ir-m]a* 8,
gana "come on": *ga-na* 1, 47, 61,
gattu "shape, figure": *gat-ti* 27,
gerru "way, path": *ge-er-ri* 65, *ge-ri* 225,
gerû "to attack, be(come) hostile": *ge-er* 61,
gêsu "to assign": *gi-is* 63, *li-gi-sak-ku* 44,
gillatu "crime, sin, transgression": *gi-il-lat* 62,
gimillu "requital, favour": *gi-mil* 66,
gimru "all": *gi-mir* 57, 60,
ginû "regular, established": *gi-na-ta-ma* 58,
gipšu "uprising, welling up": *gi-piš* 24,
girriš "like Girra, like fire": *gi-riš* 64,
gišimmaru "date palm": *gi-šim-ma-ru* 56,
habālu "to do wrong": *ha-bi-lu* 271,
halāpu "to slip into, through (clothes)": *ha-líp* 181,
halāqu "to be lost; (D) to lose, destroy": *i-hal-liq* 236, *tu-hal-li-qu* 242,
harharu "scoundrel, rascal, villain, rogue": *har-ha-ri* 221, 235, *har-ha-ru-ú* 77,
harūbu "carob (tree)": *ha-ru-bu* 186,
hasāsu "to think, mention": *ah-[su-us* 123, *tah-su-su* 61,
hašāhu "to need, desire": *ah-ši-ih* 134, *ha-šá-h[i]* 27, *tah-ši-hu* 38, 80, 145, 235, *tah-ši-ih* 65,
haššamû "superb": *ha-áš-šá-mu-u* 210,
haštu "pit, hole": *haš-tum* 62,
hašû "to crush": *i-haš-šú* 60,
hiāṭu "to check, supervise": *i-hi-ṭa* 53,
hibiltu "wrongdoing, damage": *hi-bi[l-ta]* 268,
hišihtu "requirement": *hi-ši[h-ta* 132,
hiššamû see *haššamû,*
hubur "netherworld river": *hu-bur* 17,
hubūru "a type of beer": *hu-bu[r* 224,
hurpū "early crop": *hu-ur-pi-i* 209,
hursānu "mountain": *hur-sa-an-[nu]* 211,
ibru "friend": *ib-ri* 12, 23, 265, 287, *[i]b-ri* 144,
idirtu "misery, trouble, dismay": *i-dir-tum* 12,
idu "arm, hand, example, case": *i-da-a-šú* 282, *i-da-a-tu* 243,
idû "to know": *ti-i-du* 288,
ikribu "blessing": *i[k-ri-bi]* 41,
iliš "to god, to a god": *i-liš* 54, 297,
ilku "state service, corvée": *il-ku* 74,
illu "reasoning, sense": *il-lu* 68,
illukku (a precious stone): *il-lu-uk* 57,
iltānu "north, north-wind": *il-ta-nu* 67,
iltēn "one, first": *il-te-en* 69,
iltu "goddess": *il-ti* 83, 86, *il-tim-ma* 55,
ilu "god, personal god": DINGIR 49, 66, 72, 75, 79, 80, 83, 131, 135, 219, 227, 237, 239, 240, 255, 256, 270, DINGIR-*ma* 21, 264, DINGIR.MEŠ 82, 241, 295, *i-lim* 58, *i-lu* 244, *ì-l[í]* 70,
ilūtu "divinity, godhead": DINGIR-*ti-i* 51,
ina "in": *ina* 39, 40, 64, 146, 193, 294, *i-na* 163, 177, 178, 243, 245, 246, 249, 251, 252, *i-n[a* 59,
ipšu "act, behaviour": *[i]p-šet* 145,
irītu "guidance": *i-ri-tú* 285,
ishappu "villain, rogue, incompetent": *is-hap-pu* 222, 237,
iṣu "tree": *iṣ-ṣi* 56,
išdihu "income, profit": *iš-di-[hu]* 29,
išpikku "stores (of crops), grain bin": *iš-pik-ku*

272,
ištārtu "goddess, personal goddess": ^{d}*iš-tar-t*[*i*] 73,
ištāru "goddess": ^{d}*iš-tar* 22, 40, 296, ^{d}*iš-ta-ri* 81, 132, 197, ^{d}[*iš-ta-ri*] 71,
išti "with": *iš-ti-ka* 6,
išû "to be, to have": *i-šu-ú* 24, 268, 285,
itbārtu "consortium": *it-ba-*[*ra-ti*] 294,
itti "with": *it-ti* 151,
jâši "to me": *ia-a-ši* 275,
kabāsu "to tread, tramp": *lu-ka*]*b-bi-i*[*s*] 135,
kabattu "liver, mind, mood": *kab-ta-a*[*t*]*-ka* 123, *k*]*a-bat-ta* 192, *ka-bat-ta-ka* 168, *ka-bat-tuk* 80,
kabīdu "liver": *ka-bid* 216,
kabtu "heavy, honourable, important": *kab-ti* 186, 267,
kakku "weapon, stick, mace": *kak-ka-šú* 238,
kala "all": *ka-la* 285, *ka-li-šú-nu* 222,
kalîš "all, totally": *ka-liš* 259,
kalû "to hold back": *ak-la-ma-a* 54,
kamāru "to pile up, heap up, gather": *ú-kám-mar* 22,
kamāsu "to bow": *ak-tam-sak-ku* 45, *kit-*[*m*]*u-sa-ku* 252, *kit-mu-s*[*u*] 223,
kanšu "submissive": *ka-an-šu* 166,
kânu "to be(come) established, firm, permanent": *ku-un-nam-ma-a* 33,
kapādu "to plan": *i-kap-pu-du-šú* 284, *tu-šak-pi-du* 13,
karābu "to bless, offer prayer": *ak-ru-ub* 55, *ka-ar-ba* 204,
karāṣu "to pinch off, cut": *ka-ri-iṣ* 277,
karšu "stomach; mind": *kar-šu-uk-ka* 3,
kasāsu "to gnaw, chew up": *lu-kás-si-is* 136,
kaṣāru "to bind, tie": *ka-ṣa-ru* 207,
kâša "to you": *ka-a-šá* 4,
kašāme "even though, as if": *ka-šá-me* 208,
kašāšu "to acquire": *ka-áš-šá-a-ta* 200,
katāmu "to hide, cover, overwhelm": *ka-ta-mu* 203, *ku-ut-tùm* 27,
kattû "one who guarantees, guarantor": *ak–kat-ti* 52, *ak–kat-ti-i* 49,
katû "weak, needy": *ka-ti-i* 182, 250,
katûtu "poverty": *ka-tu-ta* 75,
kî "like, how": *ki-i* 75, 82,
kibsu "track, footprint, route, mode of life": *ki-ib-si* 86,
kīdu "outside, countryside": *ki-di* 139,
kidudû "rites": *ki-du-de-e* 80,
kikurru "cella, shrine, temple": *ki-k*[*ur-r*]*i* 226,
kīma "like": *ki-ma* 256, 286,
kimiltu "anger": [*ak–k*]*i-mil-ti* 51,
kīniš "truly, genuinely, reliably, faithfully": *ki-niš* 84,
kīnu "permanent, true, reliable": *ki-i-nu* 270, *ki-na* 78, *ki-nu-te* 81,
kipdu "efforts, plan": *ki-pi-du-ši-na-ma* 85,
kittu "truth, justice, correctness": *ki-it-ta* 79, *ki-na-ti* 280,
kuāšu "to you": *ku-a-šú* 25,
kubukku "strength": *ku-bu-uk-ku* 29,
kullatu "all": *kul-lat* 200,
kumurrû "sum, total": *ku-mur-re-e* 24,
kunnû "to take care of": *ú-ka-an-nu* 269,
kuppu "cistern, water source": *ku-up-pu* 23,
kurnugû "the Land-of-No-Return": KUR.NU.GI$_4$ 10,
kūru "depression": *ku-ú-ru* 30,
kurummu "allocation, ration": *ku-ru-um* 31,
kurunnu "a kind of beer": *ku-ru-un-nu* 32,
kuṣṣudu "cripple, crippled": *ku-uṣ-ṣu-du* 76,
kušīru "profit, success": *ku-šìr-ka* 239, *ku-ši-ir* 161, *ku-ši-ri* 28,
lā "not, non-": *la* 14, 23, 24, 41, 64, 70, 74, 78, 80, 124, 145, 231, 237, 239, 257, 259, 264, 268, 274, 280, 285, *l*[*a* 190, [*l*]*a* 36, 38,
lā lē'îš "like an incompetent" *la le-'i-iš* 14,
lā lē'û "powerless, incapable": *le-e-*[*a*] 274,
lā ṭēme "senseless, meaningless" [*l*]*a ṭè-me* 36,
labānu "to point (the nose), respect, worship" *il–la-ba-an* 73,
labāšu "to dress, wear": *la-biš* 182,
labbiš "like a lion": *lab-biš* 247,
labbu "lion": *la-ba* 61, *la-bu* 50,
lakādu "to run": *i-lak-kid* 247,
lalû "beautiful thing, plenty": *la-lu* 233,
lamādu "to learn, know": *a-lam-*[*mad*] 33, *lam-da* 257, 264, *lit-mu-da* 267, *lit-mu-da-ma* 84, *li-mad* 25, 265,
lamassu "spirit, protective deity": *la-mas-*[*sa*] 21,
lāmi iṣṣūrī "fowler": *la-mi MUŠEN*.MEŠ 160,
lāmu "glowing ashes": *la-a-mi* 286,
lapānu "to be(come) poor": *il-tap-ni* 71, *la-pa-nu* 198,
lē'îš see *lā lē'îš*,
lē'û "capable": *le-'u-ú* 254, *le-'u-um* 263,
lē'ûtu "competence": *le-é-a-us-su* 257,
lemēnu "to be bad, evil, harmful": *li-it-mu-um-ma* 255, *ú-lam-ma-nu* 283,
lemnu "bad, evil, harmful": *lem-ne-ma* 220,
lemuttu "evil": *le-mut-tum* 13,
libbu "heart, mind, womb": [*l*]*i-ib-bi* 256, ŠÀ*-ba* 155, 234, ŠÀ*-ba-ka* 23, ŠÀ*-bi* 8, 203,
ligimû "kernel, sprout; youth": *il–li-gi-mi-ia-a-ma* 72, *li-gi-ma-a-šú* 128, *li-gi-mu-šá* 261,
lillidu "offspring": *li-il-li-du* 259,
lillu "idiot": *lil-li* 76, *li-il-lu* 262,
liptu "undertaking, job, creation": *li-pit* 258,
littu "cow": *li-it-tu* 260,
lū "let, may, be it": *lu* 165, 226, *lu-ú* 188, 240, 288,
lumnu "evil, action of harm": *lum-nu* 285, *lu-mun* 8,
mâ (introducing direct speech): *ma-a* 223,
ma'du "many, numerous": *ma-a'-da* 162,
madādu "to measure out, pay": *ma-di-id* 184,
mâdu "to become numerous, many": *m*[*a-a-ad*] 269,
mahāru "to face, confront, oppose": *mah-ra* 189,
mahru "front": *ma-har* 251,
makkūru "treasure, riches": *ma-ak-ku-ra* 237, *ma-ak-ku-ru* 63, *ma-qu-ru* 221,
makû "poverty": *ma-ku-ú* 27,
mala "like, as much as": *ma-a-li* 205, *ma-la* 165, 180, *ma-*[*la*] 161, *ma-la-ka* 5,
malāku "to give advice, counsel, discuss, rule": *ta-mal-lik* 200,
malālu "to eat": *ma-lil* 185,
malku "governor, ruler, king": *ma-al-ku* 64,

malû "to be(come) full; (D) to fill": *ú-ma-lu-ú* 271,
mānitu "gentle wind, breeze": *ma-nit* 67,
mannu "who, whom": *ma-an-nu* 163, 178, *ma-an-[nu]* 20,
maqātu "to fall": *ma-qit* 168, 187, *ma-[q]i-it* 160,
marāṣu "to be(come) ill, difficult": *šum-ru-ṣu* 4,
mārtu "daughter": *mar-tum* 164, *ma-[ar]-tú* 159,
māru "son": *ma-ar* 181, 182, 186, *ma-ra* 164, *ma-ru* 262,
maṣhatu "flour-offering": *maṣ-hat-s[u]* 51,
maṣṣaru "guard, watchman": *ma-aṣ-ṣar* 183,
maṣû "to match, be worth": *ma-ṣi* 261, *[i]m-ṣu* 5,
mašālu "to be equal": *tu-maš-šil* 14, *t[u-maš-šil]* 35,
mašrû "riches, wealth": *maš-re-e* 63, 75,
mātu "land": *ma-a-t[a* 179,
mērênu "naked": *mi-ri-ni-i* 182,
mēsu "cult, rites": *me-si* 81, *me-si-šu* 219,
mēšaru "justice": *mé-šá-ri* 42,
mešrû "wealth, riches": *meš-re-e* 20, 56, *meš-re-em-ma* 187, *meš-ru-ú* 282, *meš-r[u]-ú* 198,
mêšu "to scorn, disregard": *lu-meš* 135, *[te-meš]-ma* 214, *te-me-[eš]* 81,
mihiṣtu "strike, stroke (of cuneiform signs), blow, wound": *mi-hi-iṣ-ta-šú* 206,
milku "advice, counsel": *mil-[ki]* 34, *mi-lik* 58, *mi-lik-ka* 68, *mi-[lik-ka]* 45,
minsu "why?": *mìn-su* 259,
mīnu "what?": *mi-na-a* 251, 264, *mi-nu-ú* 239,
mithāriš "equally, as a whole, in the same manner": *mit-ha-riš* 18, 258,
miṭirtu "watercourse, canal, irrigation system": *miṭ-ra-ta* 245,
miṭītu "decrease, reduction": *mi-ṭi-[ta]* 24,
mūdû "learned man, knowledgeable person, specialist": *mu-du-ú* 6,
mulmullu "arrow": *mul-mul* 60,
mundalku "sage, counsellor": *m]un-dal-kúm-ma* 7,
munnerbu "fugitive, runaway": *mun-n]é-er-bu* 190,
murqu see *urqu,*
murrû "attentive(?)": *mur-ri* 259,
muššuru "(D) to release, send": *lu-maš-šìr* 138,
muštēmiqu see *emēqu,*
mutnennû "one who prays much, pious": *mut-nen-nu-ú* 289,
muttu "front part" *mut-ta-ka* 69,
mūtu "death": *mu-ú-t[u]* 16,
mutūtu "manlines": *mut-tu-t[i]* 28,
na'ādu "to pay attention, be attentive": *[l]i-'i-id* 264,
na'du "careful, attentive": *[n]a-a'-[d]u* 14,
nadānu "to give; (Št) to deliberate, ponder": *na-a[d]-nu-ma* 16, *tuš-ta-ad-di-nu* 78,
nadû "to cast, abandon": *id-da-[an]-ni* 295, *id-du-u* 160, *lu-ud-di* 133, *ta-at-ta-du-ma* 79,
nagbu "deep spring, well": *na-gab-[šú]* 23,
nagbu B "all": *na-gab* 57,
naharmumu "to break down; (Š) to cause to collapse": *uš-ha-ram-mu-šu* 286,
nahāšu "to be(come) luxuriant": *na-ha-šú* 52,
najjādu "attentive, careful": *[n]a-a-a-du* 12,
nakāsu "to cut, chop, hack": *lu-na-ak-kis* 136,
naklu "skillful, elaborate, clever": *nak-la* 212,
nakrūṭu "mercy": *nak-ru-ṭú* 44,
nammaššû "moving thing, animal": *na]m-maš-šu-u* 194,
namrāṣu "hardship, difficulty": *[n]am-ra-ṣa* 2, *nam-ra-ṣu* 288,
namru "shining, bright": *[n]a-am-ra-a* 20, *na-am-ru-tum* 15,
naparkû "to cease, stop": *ip-p]a-rak-ki* 203, *na-par-ka-a* 38,
napištu "life, vigor, breath": *nap-šat* 32, *na-piš-ti* 258,
naptanu "meal(time)": *nap-tan* 185,
naqdu "one who is in danger, critically ill": *n[a]-aq-di* 22,
narāmu "beloved one": *[n]a-ra-am* 13,
nāru "river": *na-a-ri* 17,
naṣāru "to keep watch, protect; (Š) put in safe-keeping, obey, observe": *šu-uṣ-ṣu-ru* 80, *ú-ṣur* 219, 266,
nâṣu "to despise, look down": *i-na-a-ṣa-an-ni* 253, *ta-na-ṣu* 79,
našû "to carry, hold, lift": *na-aš-šu* 218, *na-ši* 184,
naṭālu "to see, watch, observe": *a-na-aṭ-ṭ[a-al]* 293, *na-a[ṭ]-la-ta-ma* 18, *na-ṭal-šú* 19, *n[a]-ṭil* 21, *ú-ṭu-ul* 59,
ne'ellû "to roam around": *lu-ut-te-e'-lu-me* 141,
ne'û "to turn back, turn": *lu-ni-'i* 140,
nēhiš "calmly, quietly": *né-hi-iš* 291,
nēmelu "profit, gain": *né-me-li* 74,
nēmequ "wisdom": *ne-me-qí* 57, *né-me-qí* 200, *[né-m]e-qí* 47, *né-me-qú* 213,
nērtu "murder": *ner-ti* 284,
nesîš "at a distance, afar": *né-si-iš* 215,
nesû "far, distant": *né-sa-a-ti* 137,
nesû B "to be far": *né-s[a-an-ni]* 31, *né-si* 187, *né-si-ma* 256, *né-s[i-ma]* 82,
neṣû "to be strong, prevail": *né-ṣú* 58,
nešbû "satisfaction": *neš-bé-e* 31,
nēšu "lion": UR.MAH 62,
nibītu "name": *ni-bit-su* 217, 263,
nindabû "cereal offering": *nin-da-ba-a* 54,
nīru "yoke": *ni-ir* 240,
nissatu "wail, lament": *ni-is-sa-ta* 7, *ni-is-sa-tum* 30, 287,
niṣirtu "treasure": *ni-[ṣir-ta]* 271,
nišū "people": *ni-ši* 297, UN.MEŠ 18, 32, 67, 85, 129, 145, 180, 200, 257, 264, UN.[MEŠ 148,
nu'ūtu "mockery, derision": *nu-'u-ú-t[i* 230,
nullâtu "maliciousness, malicious talk": *nu-ul-la-tum* 284,
nussuqu "chosen": *nu-us-su-qa* 37, 266, *nu-us-su-qu* 68,
pakku "consideration, reasoning, sense, sagacity": *pak-ka-ka* 147, *pak-ka-ku* 35, *pak-ki* 49, 264, *pak-ku* 5,
palāhu "to be afraid of, revere": *ip-lah* 122, *pa-li-ih* 22,
palāsu "to see; (D) to direct, vision, divert attention": *[p]u-lis-su* 228,
palkû "wide, broad (an epithet used to describe scholars and scribes)": *pal-ku-ú* 254, 289, *pa[l]-ku-u* 217,

panû "to move forward, ahead": *pa-na-an-ni* 76,
pānu "front; (pl.) face": *pa-an* 21, 52, 63, *pa-ni* 275, *pa-ni-šu* 207,
pānû "former, first": *pa-na-a* 262,
parādu "to be(come) disturbed, terrified": [*ip*]-*ru-ud* 147,
parāru "to be scattered, smashed, broken up": *up-tar-ri-ir* 122,
parāsu "to cut, decide": *pa-ri-is* 244, *šu-up-ru-us* 193,
parṣu "cult, cultic order, office": *par-ṣ*[*i* 135,
parû "mule": *pa-ra-a* 248,
pasālu "to turn about, twist, obstruct": *ip-si*[*l*] 210,
paṣādu "(D) to smash, break apart": [*u*]*p-te-ṣi-id* 129,
pašallu "a type of gold": *pa-šal-lu* 271,
pašāqu "to be narrow, be(come) difficult": *šup-šu-qat-ma* 257,
patāqu "to create, form": *pa-ti-iq-ta-ši-na* 278,
paṭāru "to release": *šup-ṭu-ri* 51,
paṭû "to rejoice": *ú-paṭ-ṭa-an-ni* 206,
pehû "to block, conceal": *e-pe-ha* 125,
pêṣu "to crush, break up": [*u*]*p-te-eṣ-ṣa-am-ma* 126,
petû "to open; (D) to open, remove": *lu-up-ti* 138, *pe-ta-as-su* 62, *ú-pat-ta-a* 207,
pilludû "cultic rites": *pí-il-lu-de-e* 135,
pisnuqiš "wretchedly": *pí-is-nu-qiš* 142,
pisnuqu "feeble, wretched": *pi-is-nu-qu* 272,
pû "mouth": *pi-i* 83, *pi-ia* 34,
puhru "assembly": *pu-hur* 166, [*pu-hur* 224, *pu-hur-šú* 273, UKKIN 294,
pūhu "exchange, substitute": *pu-hi-iš* 230,
pulumku "border": [*p*]*u-lum-ku* 225,
puqqu "to pay attention, heed": [*pu-u*]*q-qa-ak* 227, *pu-u*[*q-qu*] 270, [*u*]*p-te-eq* 131,
purīdu "leg": *pu-ri-di-šú* 236,
puttû "informed, knowledgeable": [*p*]*u-tu* 226,
qablu "middle, midst": *qá-ba*[*l* 189,
qabû "to speak, say, tell": *i-qab-b*[*i* 159, *lu-u*[*q-bi-ka*] 47, [*lu*]-*uq-bi-ka* 1, *qa-ba-*[*a*] 26, *qa-bu-ú* 17, *taq-bu-ú* 12,
qadmu "pre-eminent, i.e., gods): *qad-mi* 39, *qád-mi* 251, 276,
qajjašu "generous": *qa-a-a-áš* 196,
qâlu "to pay attention": *qú-lam-ma* 26,
qamû "to burn": *i-qa-am-me-šú* 64,
qaqdâ "constantly": *qaq-dà-a* 42,
qaqqaru "ground": *qaq-qa-ri* 293,
qarānu "to pile up, heap": *qur-ru-nu* 63,
qarbatu "environs, meadowland": *qar-ba-tim* 60,
qardu "heroic": [*qa*]*r-da-ka* 43, *qar-du* 263,
qatāru "to smoke": *ú-qát-ti-ru* 30,
qatû "to come to an end": *i-qát-tu-ú* 23,
qātu "hand": ŠU 258,
qerbu "midst, centre": *qer-bi* 142, *qé-reb* 82, 246, 256, *q*]*é-reb* 211,
qerēbu "to approach, be(come) close": *qé-ru-ub* 87,
qibītu "command": *qí-bít* 83, *qí-bi-ti* 55,
rabû "big, great": *ra-bi* 247,
raggu "evil, criminal, wicked": *rag-ga* 269,
rahāṣu "to trample": *ir-hi-ṣu* 60,
ramû "to cast down, lay down": *ra-mi* 246,
rapādu "to roam, wander": [*lu-u*]*r-tap-pu-ud* 139,
râqu "to be(come) empty": *ú-raq-qu* 272,
râqu B "to be(come) far, distant": *ru-u*[*q-qan-ni*] 32,
râṣu "to rush to help": *ri-ṣa-am* 288,
rašû "to have, get, gain": *ir-ta-ši* 163, *li-ir-šá-a* 296, *ra-áš* 78, *ra-ši* 21, 237, *tu-šar-šá* 212,
rē'û "shepherd, herdsman": *re-e-um* 297,
rebītu "square, plaza": *re-bit* 291,
redû "to follow, pursue": *i-red-di* 248, *i-red-di-šu* 238, *re-dan-n*[*i*] 275, *ri-di-ma* 219,
rēmēnû "compassionate": *re-me-na-at* 287,
rēmu "mercy": *re-ma* 296,
rêmu "to have mercy": *i-rem-mu* 41,
rēšiš "like a slave": *re-šiš* 294,
rēštû "first": *reš-tu-ú* 260,
rēšu "head": *re-eš* 216, *re-e-šú* 289, *re-ši* 218, *re-ši-ia* 293,
riābu "to replace, restore": *ta-rab* 242,
riddu "guidance, common sense": [*ri-id* 220, *ri-id-di* 214,
rigmu "noise, scream": *ri-ig-mu* 292,
ripittu "straying, errancy": *ri-pi-it-ta* 212,
rīṣu "help": *ri-ṣa* 290, 295,
ritpāšu "very wide": *rit-pa-šu* 234,
ru'u "friend": [*ru-'u*]-*ú-a* 45,
rubû "prince": NUN 226, *ru-bi-i* 185,
rukūbu "vehicle": *ru-ku-ub* 210,
rūqu "distant": *ru-uq-m*[*a*] 201,
ruššû "red gold": *ru-uš-ši-i* 184,
sabāsu "to be(come) angry" *sa-ba-sa* 39,
sadāru "to place in order, do regularly" *sa-di-ir* 240,
sadru "in order, regular": *sa-ad-ri* 35,
sagû "ritual; cella": *sa-ga-a* 84,
sahāru "to go around, seek, turn": *as-h*[*u-ur*] 72, *i-s*[*ah-hur*] 39, *li-sah-h*[*ir*] 297, *su-hu*[*r*] 42,
sahhu "meadow": *sah-hi-ka* 13, *sa-hi-ia* 31,
salmu "peaceful": *sa-lit-*[*t*]*um* 40,
samîš "like one undecided": *sa-miš* 37,
samku "buried": *sa-am-ku* 41,
sanninu "obstinate, tenacious": *sa-an-ni-nu* 43,
sanqu "checked": *sa-an-qa* 34,
santakku "triangle, wedge; regularly, always, continuously": *sa-an-tak-ku* 38, 280,
saphu "scattered, dispersed": [*sa-a*]*p-hu* 36,
sarriš "falsely": *sar-ri-iš* 285,
sarru "false, criminal": *sar-ra-a-ti* 280,
sattukku "regular delivery, regular offering": *sat-tuk-ku* 55,
serremu "onager": *ser-re-mu* 59, *sér-re-mu* 48,
siqru "word, speech, command": *sè-qar* 46, 266,
sulû "street, lane": *su-le-e* 141, 209,
suppû "to pray, petition; supplication, petition": *su-up-pe-e* 39, *ú-sap-p*[*a*] 54,
sūqu "street, suq": *su-qí* 249,
surru see *ana surri*,
ṣabû "to wish": *ṣa-bu-u-šu* 218,
ṣâdu "to prowl, roam, turn": *a-ṣa-a-ád* 209, *i-ṣa-a-a-ad* 249, *lu-ṣa-a-*[*a-ad*] 141,
ṣāriru "flashing red gold": *ṣa-ri-ra* 183, *ṣa-ri-ri* 53,
ṣēru "back, open country, steppe": EDIN 59, 162, EDIN] 59,
ṣurru "interior, heart": *ṣur-ra-ka* 212, 255, *ṣur-*

ri-k[*a* 146,
ša "that; which; who": *ša* 74, 233, 234, 235, 237, 239, 242, *šá* 4, 12, 23, 24, 38, 48, 50, 52, 61, 63, 66, 71, 78, 125, 156, 160, 162, 166, 223, 225, 231, 235, 241, 251, 263, 267, 268, 269, 270, 271, 272, 273, 281, 295, 296, [*šá* 46,
šadādu "to drag, carry, pull": *i-šad-da-ad* 245, *ša-di-id* 240,
šadû "mountain": *šá-du-ú* 34,
šagāšu "to murder": *šá-ga-š*[*á*] 267,
šaggāšu "murderer": *ša-ga-šu* 238,
šakānu "to place, establish": *il-ta-kan* 75, *liš-ku-nu* 295, *liš-ku-u*[*n*] 43, *na-áš-kin* 220, *šit-kun* 216,
šalāmu "to be(come) well, healthy, intact": *šal-ma-a*[*t* 152,
šalbābu "wise": *šal-ba-ba* 204,
šalṭu "authoritative, having authority": *šal-ṭu* 273,
šamhu "luxuriant, lush": *šam-hu* 253,
šammû (mng. uncert., probably "vitality"): *ša-am-mé-e* 236,
šamšu "sun": ᵈUTU-*ši* 297,
šamû "the heavens": AN-*e* 82, 256,
šanānu "to equal, vie": *iš-šá-nin* 6,
šanû "second, next, other, different": *šá-ni-i* 263, *šá-ni-t*[*ú*] 195,
šanû A "to do for a second time; (D) to repeat, do twice, report, recount": [*l*]*u-šá-an-ni-ka* 2,
šanû B "(Gt) to be(come) different": *šit-na-a* 243,
šapālu "to be(come) low; (D) to make lower, humiliate": *at-taš-pil* 77, *iš-šá-pil* 292, *šá-pil-ma* 260, *ú-šap-pa-lu* 268,
šaplu "bottom": *šá-pal* 252,
šaptu "lip": *šap-ta-a-a* 204,
šapû "to be(come) dense, loud": *iš-šá-pu* 292,
šaqû "to be(come) high": *il-ta-qu-ú* 77, *ú-šá-áš-qu-ú* 267,
šarāku "to present, bestow": *iš-ru-ku-šú* 280, *i-šar-ra-ak* 250, *šar-ku* 279, *šar-ku-uš* 284,
šarbābiš "impotently": *šar-ba-bi-iš* 286,
šarhiš "proudly": *šar-hi-iš* 281,
šarhu "noble, proud, honourable": *šar-hu* 277,
šarrabu "a demon": *šar-ra-bi* 244,
šarrāqiš "like a robber": *šar-ra-qiš* 283, [*šar*]-*ra-qiš* 139,
šarratu "queen": *šar-ra-tum* 278,
šarru "king": LUGA[L]-*ri* 210, *šar-ma* 282, *šar-ri* 276, *š*[*a*]*r-ri* 181,
šarû "rich; to be(come) rich": *šá-ri-i* 186, 281, *šá-ru-ú* 253, *ú-šá-áš-re-*[*e*] 19,
šāru "wind, breeze": *ša-a-ra* 241,
šassūru "womb": *šá-sur-ra* 150,
šāt "those who, those which": *ša-at* 232,
šattu "year, harvest time": MU.AN.NA 242,
šâṭu "to draw, pull yoke": *a-šá-aṭ* 74,
še'û "to seek": *e-še-'e* 73, *muš-te-'u-u* 70, *ši-te-'e-e* 66, *ši-te-'e-e-ma* 241, *ši-te-'e-me* 287,
šemû "to hear": *iš-š*[*e-em-me*] 83, *ši-me* 26,
šētu "web": [*še-e-ti*] 160,
šêtu "to miss": *še-te-ku* 28,
šibqū "scheme, plan, idea": *šib-qí* 82, *ši-ib-qí-i*[*a*] 265,
šību "old man, elder": *ši-bu* 223,
šīmtu "fate": *š*[*i*]*m-tum* 9, *ši-ma-ti* 64,
šīru "flesh, meat, body": *ši-r*[*i*] 50,
šittīn "twice, two thirds": *šit-tin-šu* 261,
šu'ētu "lady, mistress": *šu-e-tú* 278,
šu'û "master, lord": *šu-'e-e* 254, *šu-'u-ú* 188,
šubultu "ear of barley": *šu-b*[*u-la-tú*] 48,
šuhhû "to remove": *šúh-hu-ú* 215,
šukāmu "scribal art": *šu-ka-mi* 205,
šummu "edict, law": *šu-um-mu* 198, *šum-me* 214,
šumu "name": *šum-šu* 161, *šu-um* 190,
šūquru "superb, extraordinary": *šu-qu-ru* 167,
šūt "who, those who": *šu-ut* 189,
tabīnu "shelter, stall": *ta-*[*b*]*i-na* 226,
tahanātu "help": *ta-ha-na-at* 43,
tâmtu "sea": *tam-tim* 24,
tamû "to swear": *ta-mu-u* 188,
tappû "companion, partner": *tap-pu-ú* 2,
tārû "child-minder, fosterer": *ta-ru-u-a* 11,
târu "to turn": *i-ta-ar* 10, *i-ta-ri* 40, *lut-t*[*i-ir*] 69,
tašīmtu "discernment, sagacity": *ta-šim-ti* 254, *ta-šim-tú* 199,
tēmēqu "prayer, benediction": *te-me-qí* 73,
terdennu "younger, second(ary)": *ter-den-nu* 250,
ti'ûtu "nourishment, sustenance": *ti-'u-ut-*[*su*] 272, *ti-ú-ta* 250,
tukultu "trust, help": *tuk-la-tum* 290,
tupšikku "brick-carrying frame, brick hod, earth basket": *tup-šik-ku* 215,
ṭābu "pleasant, good, gratifying": *ṭa-a-ba* 241 *ṭa-a-*[*bu*] 67,
ṭapālu "to slander, insult": *ta-aṭ-pil* 214,
ṭapāpiš "for satiation, contentment": *ṭa-pa-piš* 32,
ṭapāpu "to be very full": *iṭ-pu-pu* 48,
ṭarādu "to send off, send away, dispatch": *tu-ṭar-rid* 213, *ú-ṭa-ra-du* 270,
ṭēmu "decision, reasoning, sense": *ṭè-em* 72, 239, 270, *ṭè-*[*em* 227, *ṭè-en-ga* 67, 167, *ṭè-en-ka* 14, *ṭè-en-ši-na* 87, *ṭè-me* 36,
ṭiṭṭu "clay": *ṭi-iṭ-ṭa-ši-na* 277,
ṭuhdu "abundance, wealth": *ṭuh-*[*da*] 22,
ṭuppu "tablet": *ṭu*]*p-p*[*a-ni*] 205,
u "and, but": *u* 11, 30, 73, 164, 182, 198, 253, 280, 290, *ú* 275, *ù* 186, 220,
ugum (mng. obscure): *ú-gu-um* 154,
ukkuliš "very dark": *uk-ku-liš* 15,
ukkupiš "very early, near": *uk-ku-piš* 208,
ukultu "food, consumption": *uk-*[*lat-su*] 186,
ul "not": *ul* 83, 203, 244, 290, 292, 293, 294,
ulālu "weak, powerless, helpless": *ú-la-la* 274,
ulla "ancient time": *ul-la* 17,
ullilu "anyone": *ul-li-*[*l*]*u-ú* 19,
ullû "ancient time, distant time": *u*[*l-li*]*-im* 198,
ultu "since, from": *ul-tu* 17, *ul-tú* 198,
ūmu "day": UD-*mu* 33, 191, UD-*um* 64,
urhu "path": *ú-ru-uh* 16, 70, 208, *ú-ru-uh-šu* 247,
urqu "green; sense, reason": *mur-qa* 78, *ur-qa-ka* 37,
uršu "wisdom": *u*[*r-ši*] 57,
usandû "fowler": *ú-sa-an-di-i* 202,
ūsu "good practice, usage, custom": *us* 219,
uṣṣuṣu "to investigate, question": *lu-uṣ-ṣi-iṣ-ka* 25,

uṣurtu "plan": *ú-ṣur-ti* 79,
uznu "ear, wisdom": *uz-ni* 78, *ú-zu-un-šu* 49,
zamar "soon, right now": *za-mar* 236, 290,
zārû "begetter, progenitor": *za-ru-ú* 9, 245,
zikru "word, speech, command": *zik-ra* 69,
zilullîš "like a vagrant, tramp": *zi-lul-li*[*š*] 249,
zīmu "appearance, face": *zi-mu-ka* 15, *zi-mu-*[*ú-a*] 30,

Index of Names

Divine Names

SIGN LIST

001	*aš*	1
	ina	6
	ṭil	1
002	*ḫal*	2
003	*muq*	1
005	*ba*	35
	BA	1
006	*ṣú*	1
	zu	3
007	*su*	23
009	*bal*	3
	pal	4
010	*ád*	1
012	*ḫaš*	2
	ḫaz	1
	sil	1
	šil	2
	tar	6
	ṭar	1
013	*an*	29
	d	16
	AN	3
	DINGIR	23
015	*ka*	61
035	*nak*	2
038	URU	1
040	UKKIN	1
049*	U_{18}	1
053	*šiḫ*	1
	šúḫ	1
055	*la*	53
	LA	1
057	*maḫ*	1
	MAḪ	1
058	*tu*	22
	ṭú	1
059	*le*	10
	li	31
060	*kúr*	2
061	*mu*	26
	MU	1
062	*qa*	11
068	*ru*	51
	šup	2
069	*bat*	3
	be	3
	bít	1
	mid	1
	mit	2
	miṭ	1
	tel	1
	til	1
070	*na*	71
	NA	1
072	*kul*	1
073	*ti*	47
	TI	1
074	*mas*	1
	maṣ	1
	maš	6
	BAR	1
075	*nu*	41
	NU	1
077	*kun*	1

078	*ḫu*	19
	pak	5
	MUŠEN	1
079	*nam*	4
	NAM	1
080	*eq*	2
	ig	1
	ik	1
	iq	4
081	*mut*	4
084	*zi*	5
085	*ge*	3
	gi	14
086	*dal*	2
	re	20
	ri	61
	ṭal	1
	RI	1
087	*ṣil*	1
	zil	1
	NUN	1
088	*kab*	4
	kap	1
090	*gat*	1
	kat	2
094	*tim*	3
095	*mun*	3
097	*ag*	1
	ak	15
	aq	4
099	*en*	9
	EN	4
101	*sur*	4
104	*sa*	25
111	*qur*	1
112	*si*	8
114	*dar*	1
115	*reš*	1
	riš	3
	sak	2
	šak	1
122	MÁ	1
123	*dir*	1
124	*tap*	3
126	*šum*	3
	tak	3
	taq	3
128	*ab*	3
	ap	3
129	*nap*	2
129a	*mul*	3
130	*uk*	7
	uq	7
131	*as*	2
	aṣ	2
134	*um*	9
138	*dub*	1
	dup	1
	tup	1
	ṭup	1
139	*ta*	57
142	*i*	72
	I	1
142a	*ia*	9
143	*kám*	1
	kan	1

	qan	1
	GAN	1
144	TUR	1
145	*ad*	9
	at	11
	aṭ	4
147	*ṣi*	5
148	*in*	2
149	*rab*	1
151	LUGAL	1
152	*ḫir*	2
	sar	2
	šar	14
	šìr	2
164	*sè*	2
167	*gab*	2
	qab	1
	ṭuḫ	1
168	EDIN	3
169	*taḫ*	6
170	*am*	9
172	*bil*	3
	kúm	1
	ne	2
	pil	4
	ṭè	9
183	*ram*	1
190	*zik*	1
191	*qu*	14
205	*il*	23
206	*du*	18
207	*dum*	4
	tum	15
211	*nit*	1
	uš	3
	UŠ	1
212	*iš*	26
	mil	3
214	*bé*	7
	bi	24
	kás	1
	pí	2
	BI	1
215	*šim*	4
230	*dà*	1
	kak	1
	qaq	2
231	*ì*	1
	lí	1
	né	13
	ni	30
232	*er*	4
	ir	9
233	*mal*	1
295	*ḫat*	1
	pa	22
	PA	1
295k	*sap*	1
	šap	2
296	*eṣ*	1
	is	12
	iṣ	5
	iz	1
	GIŠ	3
298	*al*	5

306	*ub*	10
	up	9
	UB	2
307	*mar*	4
	MAR	1
308	*e*	37
309	*lud*	1
	lut	2
312	*un*	5
	UN	11
313	*kid*	1
	kit	2
	qit	2
	saḫ	3
314	*lak*	4
	miš	1
	red	2
	rid	1
	rit	1
	šet	1
	šit	4
318	*šam*	1
	ú	84
319	*ga*	12
	qá	1
322	*dan*	2
	kal	1
	lab	1
	líp	1
	reb	4
	tan	1
324	*bid*	1
	bit	3
	é	1
	pit	1
325	*ner*	1
326	GI$_4$	1
328	*ra*	34
330	LÚ	1
331	*šiš*	2
333	*qar*	5
334	*ed*	1
	et	2
	id	8
	it	9
	iṭ	2
	ID	1
335	*da*	19
	ṭa	8
336	*lil*	2
339	*áš*	13
342	*ma*	87
	MA	4
346	*biš*	3
	piš	4
	qer	1
347	*mir*	3
349	*bur*	2
353	*ša*	12
354	*qad*	1
	qád	2
	qat	1
	qát	2
	šu	51
	ŠU	1
355	*lul*	2
	nar	1
	LUL	1
362	*qam*	1

366	*kur*	1
	lad	1
	lat	3
	mad	3
	mat	1
	sat	1
	šad	1
	šat	1
	KUR	1
367	*še*	6
371	*bu*	29
	pu	21
	sér	1
	BU	2
372	*us*	7
	uṣ	4
	uz	2
373	*ser*	1
374	*muš*	2
	ṣir	1
375	*ter*	3
376	*te*	27
	TE	1
377	*kar*	1
378	*lis*	1
	liš	7
381	*laḫ*	1
	par	2
	tam	2
	tú	11
	ud	3
	ut	6
	TÚ	1
	UD	3
	UTU	1
383	*pe*	3
	pi	8
384	*šà*	1
	ŠÀ	5
396	*ḫi*	14
397	*ʾe*	5
	ʾi	4
	ʾu	9
	aʾ	2
	eʾ	3
398	*aḫ*	2
	eḫ	1
	iḫ	3
	uḫ	4
399	*em*	6
	im	2
401	*ḫar*	4
	ḫur	6
	mur	5
411	*u*	17
	U	1
420	*lit*	4
425	*kis*	1
	kiš	1
	qiš	3
427	*mé*	4
	mi	22
434	*tùm*	1
435	*lam*	6
437	*ṣur*	6
	ZUR	1
441	*ul*	18
449	*lem*	1
	lim	1
	ši	34
451	*ar*	8

455		*ù*	2
457		*de*	2
		di	14
		ṭi	3
461		*ki*	21
		qé	5
		qí	14
465		*den*	1
		tin	1
467		*dun*	3
469		*pat*	1
		paṭ	1
471		*mìn*	1
		neš	1
		niš	2
472		*eš*	3
480		*ana*	8
481		*lal*	1
483		*ḫap*	2
		rem	1
		rin	1
491		*ṣar*	1
511		*ḫap*	2
532		*me*	21
		šib	1
533		*meš*	7
		MEŠ	15
535		*eb*	1
		ep	1
		ib	12
		ip	5
		IB	5
536		*ku*	53
		qú	2
		tuš	1
		KU	1
537		*dab*	1
		lu	49
		LU	1
538		*kin*	1
		qi	1
545		*šú*	30
554		*rag*	1
		rak	1
		raq	1
		šal	4
555		*ṣu*	9
556		*nen*	1
		nin	2
557		*dam*	2
559		*gu*	3
564		*el*	1
565		*lum*	4
574		*tuk*	3
575		*lik*	6
		liq	1
		taš	1
		tíš	1
		ur	6
		UR	1
579		*a*	129
		A	1
586		*ṣa*	13
		za	6
589		*ḫa*	14
592		*pik*	1
		šik	1

595	𒌅	*ṭu*	3
597	𒊭	*šá*	69

www.ingramcontent.com/pod-product-compliance
Lightning Source LLC
Chambersburg PA
CBHW041143120626
46547CB00020B/3089
* 9 7 8 9 5 2 1 0 1 3 4 3 0 *